The Secret of Abundant Living

BY Charles L. Allen

God's Psychiatry
The Touch of the Master's Hand
All Things Are Possible Through Prayer
When You Lose a Loved One
The Twenty-Third Psalm
Healing Words
Twelve Ways to Solve Your Problem
The Life of Christ
Prayer Changes Things
The Sermon on the Mount
Life More Abundant
The Charles L. Allen Treasury (Charles Wallis)
When You Graduate (with Mouzon Biggs)
The Miracle of Love
The Miracle of Hope
The Miracle of the Holy Spirit
What I Have Lived By
Christmas (with Charles L. Wallis)
You Are Never Alone
In Quest of God's Power
Perfect Peace
How to Increase Your Sunday-School Attendance
    (with Mildred Parker)
The Secret of Abundant Living

Charles L. Allen

The Secret of Abundant Living

Fleming H. Revell Company
Old Tappan, New Jersey

Library of Congress Cataloging in Publication Data

Allen, Charles Livingstone,
The secret of abundant living.

1. Self-love (Theology)   2. Self-acceptance.
3. Christian life—Methodist authors.   I. Title.
BV4639.A384   248.4   80-17524
ISBN 0-8007-1123-8

Contents

Preface: Begin by Loving Yourself   13

1 **Learn to Love Yourself**   15

    Overcoming Self-hatred
    Three Steps to Self-love
    Be Somebody
    You Are a You—Not an "It"
    The Legend of the Three Trees
    Love Is One Package
    Love Demands Interest

2 **What Do You Think of Yourself?**   29

    What Is Man?
    Fellowship
    Where Are We Going?
    Dreams Are They . . .

3 **Do Not Be Ashamed of Yourself**   35

    A Touch of Phoniness in Us All
    The Basic Facts About You
    There Is Only One of Each of Us
    See a Picture of Yourself
    Sing the Note You Can Sing

4 **The Problem of Finding Out the Person You Really Are**   40

    The Power to Become
    Four Affirmations

8

Critical or Complimentary?

5 **When One Feels Not Counted** 43

We *Do* Count
God Knows Your Name
You Are Significant
The Indispensable Man
Karl Downs?

6 **Take the Responsibility for Yourself** 49

Two Questions
Your Own Policeman
Our Money
Our Hearts
Our Minds
Our Tongues

7 **Personal Power Comes From a Purpose** 61

Life Is a Journey
Keep Going
Do Not Be Discouraged
A Five-Year Plan

8 **Learn to Believe, Dream, and Ask** 67

A Multitalented Boy
A Man Who Loved
Who Was This Man?
Life's Six Great Moments
Dreams Have No Limit

9 **Do Not Be Afraid to Ask** 72

It's in the Scriptures
Fourteen Degrees
Four Principles in Asking
First Four Letters of the Alphabet

9

10 **Try Asking God** 80

When We Don't Receive
A Right Relationship
God Knows When to Answer
Have Patience

11 **Quotients** 86

Drive Quotient
Creativity Quotient
Awareness Quotient
Patience Quotient
Love Quotient
Teach Me to Love

12 **Past, Present, Future** 89

The Road Not Taken
Today Is Tomorrow's Yesterday
We Are Not Alone
536,870,912 Pennies
The Stone

13 **Failures Are Never Final** 100

Win or Lose
"He Simply Got Up and Left"
Let Your Anchor Down
"Then Laugh"
Don't Turn Back

14 **Pain Is Pain** 107

You Cannot Explain It
It Is Not the Circumstance: It Is You
Responsibility for Ourselves
Our Real Resources

15 **The Cure for an Inferiority Complex** 112

Six Wrong Methods
Three Good Methods

"Your Moment Has Come"

16 You Can Be What You Want to Be   **118**
Wise Advice
Start Now
Conditions for Becoming a Whole Person
A Special Rock
The Principles of Being the Person You Can Be

**17 You Never Find Happiness Through
Searching for It**   **123**
Keeping on the Move
"Me-First" People
Signs of a Happy Person

18 Be the Boss of Your Habits   **126**
Six Basic Steps
Greatest Accomplishment in Life
Four Kinds of Habits

19 That Complex We Call Inferiority   **130**
Inferiority Cover-ups
Reasons for an Inferiority Complex
How to Grow in Adequacy
What We Want the Most

20 Finalize Your Fear   146   **136**
Test Your Fears
Paranoia—Euphoria—Metanoia
Biblical Example
Fear Can Be Conquered

21 Spite, Jealousy, and Self-pity   **142**
Liking to Be Liked
Importance of Solitude
A Scapegoat
Understanding Acceptance

22 Learn to Get Along With Others   **146**

    Three Attitudes
    Tensions in Marriage
    Be Interested
    Importance of Listening
    What Are Your Interests?
    A Personality Interest Checklist
    Rules for Getting Along With Other People

Conclusion: Why Jesus Came   **154**

Preface:

Begin by Loving Yourself

Jesus never beat people over the head to make them better. If someone needed help, He did not condemn them; instead He reached out in a spirit of loving concern. So we are not surprised to read, "Then drew near unto him all the publicans and sinners for to hear him " (Luke 15:1).

For many years I have been the minister of a church in the center of a big city. In addition, I have spoken in many, many places. I just cannot count the people I have talked to across the years. It is my deep feeling that the major problem of people is that they do not have a high enough opinion of themselves. They feel guilt and shame, and unworthiness and inadequacy. Feeling these emotions, many people run from life and never live up to their best. In these pages I have sought to lift up the words of Christ, "Thou shalt love the Lord, thy God. . . . Thou shalt love thy neighbour as thyself" (Matthew 22:37, 39). I think true love begins by loving ourselves. If we do not have the right opinion of ourselves, then we will not properly love either God or other people. Over and over in these pages I keep saying, "Love thyself."

Through the years I have kept a file of quotations, poems, and inspirational material. Sometimes I do not have the proper source for some of this material; it is my intention always to give credit, but when I do not give proper credit, it is because I do not know where to give it. I certainly am grateful to many people whose writings have inspired me.

I especially appreciate the Fleming H. Revell Company for so much help in publishing all of my books. Mrs. Constance

Ward, my secretary for many years, helps me greatly and to her I owe a great debt.

CHARLES L. ALLEN
FIRST UNITED METHODIST CHURCH
1320 MAIN STREET
HOUSTON, TEXAS 77002

The Secret of Abundant Living

1
Learn to Love Yourself

Love yourself.

To many people that seems to be a totally wrong concept, and certainly the thought of loving yourself, in the minds of many, is utterly unchristian. Fixed in our minds are the words of Jesus, " . . . If any man will come after me, let him deny himself, and take up his cross, and follow me" (Matthew 16:24). We say with Paul, "I am crucified with Christ . . . " (Galatians 2:20). Also we quote Paul with approval, " . . . I die daily" (1 Corinthians 15:31).

Many people fix in their minds that living the highest life means being dead to themselves—giving themselves—forgetting themselves—losing their lives—suffering for a cause—and on and on. It has been said over and over, "God first, others second, yourself last." Within the right interpretation, all of these expressions are valid and most acceptable.

However, let us remember that Jesus agreed with the lawyer who said, " . . . Thou shalt love the Lord thy God with all thy heart, and with all thy soul, and with all thy strength, and with all thy mind; and thy neighbour as thyself" (Luke 10:27). When we read those words, we are so impressed with the forceful emphasis on our love for God and the fact that next our neighbor is mentioned, that we really miss the key to that entire great statement. Those last two words should be written in bold, capital letters: **AS THYSELF!** That is where it all begins. Our attitudes and feelings toward God and others begin with our attitudes and feelings toward ourselves. *One:* If you hate yourself, you hate other people, and you hate God. *Two:* If you do not care about yourself, you do not care about other people, and you do not care about God. *Three:* If you love yourself, you love other people, and you love God. The beginning of the whole business of love is *learning to love yourself.*

The precept that our attitudes begin with ourselves is beautifully expressed in a poem entitled "A Life in Your Hands."

> If a child lives with criticism,
>   He learns to condemn,
> If a child lives with hostility,
>   He learns to fight,
> If a child lives with ridicule,
>   He learns to be shy,
> If a child lives with shame,
>   He learns to feel guilty,
> If a child lives with tolerance,
>   He learns to be patient,
> If a child lives with encouragement,
>   He learns confidence,
> If a child lives with praise,
>   He learns to appreciate,
> If a child lives with fairness,
>   He learns justice,
> If a child lives with security,
>   He learns to have faith,
> If a child lives with approval,
>   He learns to like himself,
> If a child lives with acceptance and friendship,
>   He learns to find love in the world.
>   DOROTHY LAW HOLTE

Never get the idea that loving yourself means excluding others. Genuine self-love is never egocentricity or selfishness. Loving yourself does not mean that you are seeking as much as possible out of life—and willing to give as little as possible. Neither is self-love, pride, arrogance, a sense of superiority, or, an exaggerated feeling of importance. True self-love is mirrored in our attitude toward God and our fellowman. We look at others through the attitudes that we have toward ourselves. "Learn to love yourself" is really the starting place.

Overcoming Self-hatred

Not only should we be concerned about our attitudes toward God and other people, but in learning to love ourselves, we overcome the damaging emotion of self-hatred. Remembering some bad decision, we say, "I could kick myself for being so stupid." We look back on actions in some yesterday with shame and remorse and deep guilt. We cannot forget—we refuse to forgive. Instead, we relive and rethink, over and over, some wrong we did, until we think ourselves into despair and self-degradation.

There are many other reasons why people hate themselves, such as, discrimination they have received because of their race, or color, or national origin. We depreciate ourselves because we lack the talents someone else possesses. Some people do not have the education that they wanted and they need, and they mourn over opportunities that are now gone.

Learn to love yourself in order to stop hating yourself.

We transfer to others the attitude we have toward ourselves. Loving ourselves, we wish good for other people. Hating ourselves, we want others pulled down to our level. Not being happy with ourselves, we are not happy with anybody else.

It has been well said:

> When folks is mean, it ain't that they hate you personal. It's more likely because they are miserable about something in their inside. You got to remember how most of the time when they yell at you or get after you, it ain't you they are yelling at but something inside themselves you never even heard tell of, like some other person has been mean to them, or something they

hoped for didn't come true, or they done something
they are ashamed even to think of, so they get mad at
you just to keep their minds off it.

Boy George in "The Foolkiller"

The truth of the matter is, just for our own self-preservation,
we need to learn to love ourselves. Hating ourselves: one, dis-
torts our personalities; two, blocks all happiness out of our
lives; three, creates within us negative spirits; four, makes us
cynical, complaining, and contentious; and five, ruins all of our
relationships with God and our fellowman.

Notice that we are told to "learn to love ourselves." It is not
something that comes with just a quick decision. You do not
simply say, "I will start loving myself," and find it accomplished. If you wish to play the piano, it takes learning; if you
wish to paint beautiful pictures, it takes learning. So it is with
loving ourselves.

Three Steps to Self-love

Being convinced that we need to learn to love ourselves,
there are three steps to take, but these steps are neither small,
nor are they simple.

First, we must learn to love God. This seems a contradiction
of what we have just been saying, but the truth of the matter
is, the beginning of self-love is self-forgetting. Our very beginning is in God, and we can love God because the Bible tell us,
"We love him, because he first loved us" (1 John 4:19). Love for
God does not originate within us; rather it is response to God.
He made the world in which we live. He causes the sun to shine
and all of creation to keep going. More importantly, God knows
each person by name. We make great progress when we realize
that God's love does not begin with *mankind,* but with each
individual. If God did not love even just one person, then His
love for mankind would be incomplete and imperfect.

When one person—any person—every person—realizes that he or she is God's child, does that person dare to hate God's child? In the second place, *we love God because He takes out of our lives the wrong, negative attitudes we have toward ourselves.* Self-hatred, a sense of guilt, a feeling of unworthiness, the realization of past mistakes and sin—all these and more— God forgives and forgets. The Bible says, " . . . for thou hast cast all my sins behind thy back" (Isaiah 38:17).

When God forgives, sin is gone out of sight and is remembered no more. When God forgives, no person needs to hate self any longer. If God is willing to take us into His loving fellowship, then we can live with ourselves in that same loving fellowship.

The third step is *through fellowship with God.* We realize we are not dependent just on our own selves. We are not alone; we have a fellowship which empowers. We stop saying such things as, "This is beyond me and my abilities." Instead, we begin saying with Paul, "I can do all things through Christ which strengtheneth me" (Philippians 4:13).

When we think of our own littleness, we are constantly defeating ourselves. When we think of the greatness of God, we have confident assurance. We can handle the job that is ours to do. We can make friends; we can face troubles; we can quit hating ourselves. Never forget that God is on the side of success. God is never a party to failure.

So to begin with, in loving God, we come to love ourselves, and through loving ourselves, we can love all mankind.

Be Somebody

Through the years, I have received far more pay for my work than I deserve. Early one morning I got on an airplane in another state to come home from a speaking engagement. I was sleepy and tired, and I just wanted to rest. Sitting beside me, however, was one of those talking people, and he kept it up, until we arrived at the airport where I was to change planes to come on home. During that trip he asked my name, my occupation, and repeated what I said in a voice loud enough for every person in a good area of the plane to hear it all. I felt embarrassed and happy to be leaving that brother. As I walked off the plane, a man who was sitting just in front of me waited at the door until I got there. Then he told me that twenty-six years ago, I had spoken in chapel in the high school where he was a student. He explained to me that his father worked in a cotton mill, and they lived in a cotton-mill community. He felt unworthy and almost hopeless. I spoke that morning on the subject "Be Somebody." Somehow, he explained, my words got into his mind to the point that he came to believe that he *could* be somebody. Then he said to me, "I am now the minister of the largest church of my denomination in my state. I would never be what I am had I not decided that I could 'be somebody.'"

On the way home I tried to remember what I said in that twenty-minute speech about being somebody. But I could not remember it. The truth is, I do not even remember making the speech. As long as I live, I will thank God for that minister who spoke to me. It makes me feel grateful to God that He chose me as an instrument to speak to that high-school boy.

I wish I could say to every person, "Be somebody." The truth is, you *are* somebody.

I like the story of the lady who met a little boy and asked him his name.

He replied, "My name is George Washington."

"I hope that you grow up to be like George Washington," the lady said.

"I cannot help being like George Washington, because that is who I am," was the boy's reply.

You Are a You—Not an "It"

In the "Christmas Oratorio" by W. H. Auden, you read, ".... remembering the stable where for once in our lives, everything became a you and nothing was an it." That is a glorious phrase. It is wonderful to know that the *its* in society were turned into *yous*. No person is an *it;* every person is a *you*. The ministry of Jesus was spent making this change possible for: lepers; a woman with a bent back; one who was about to be stoned to death; a tax gatherer; a man sitting in a sycamore tree; a lame man beside a pool—the misfits of society. Even to the thief on the cross, He said, " . . . To day shalt thou be with me in paradise" (Luke 23:43). In some translations of the Bible, the word *thou* is translated *you*. We can say that Jesus was turning a man who admitted that he was being justly put to death into a *you*. The word *thou* has a sacredness about it to many of us—even beyond *you*. If He could do it for that man, He can do it for any person.

Not just the outcast, however, was Jesus interested in. Such men as the prominent, wealthy Joseph of Arimathea and the rich young ruler also came within His concern. Every person is a *you*—even a *thou*.

The more you study this world, the surer you become that everything has significance. For example, an apple falling from a tree may seem utterly unimportant—except that when Isaac Newton saw it, he made the discovery of the law of gravity. It unlocked untold numbers of scientific doors for the good of mankind.

Every morning in many homes a teakettle on the stove begins to boil. For most of us, the boiling water simply means a cup of tea or a cup of coffee. To Robert Fulton it meant the principle of the steam engine. This invention literally made possible so much of the industry which has developed our society.

We need to learn that there is no insignificant moment or experience and—most importantly—*person*.

A researcher, in studying the history of the Adams family, came across the diary of Charles Francis Adams. He found that for a certain day the only words recorded were, WENT FISHING WITH SON. DAY WASTED. The son was named Brooks Adams, and in his writing, he referred to that day which he had spent fishing with his father. He described how the fish were not biting and how they did not catch even one. Instead, they sat talking. Brooks was only twelve years old at the time, but he asked his father many questions, and his illustrious father explained to him many of the important aspects of life. Later on, Brooks Adams, in recalling that day, said, "This was the most significant changing point in my life."

For one, it was "day wasted." For another it was "life-changing."

There are really no insignificant events, no wasted days, and *no* unimportant people.

The Legend of the Three Trees

Each time I read "The Legend of the Three Trees" I get a new joy and an inspiration. It goes like this:

In the shadows of our far-distant past on the slopes of the mountain of the Jordan Valley, there stood three trees. One sunny day, when all the world looked peaceful and in harmony, they were discussing their destinies.

"Ah," said the first tree, "I have long thought of my wishes for the future. I hope to be hauled down these mountains and into the city of Jerusalem, and there to be cut up and made into a beautiful paneling for the Temple. How I could be of service to God, if only that would occur! For think how many men and women would come to the Temple to worship, and see my beautiful grain, and be helped to understand how majestic is the God who created me!"

"Well, my desire," said the second tree, "is to serve men and women. I hope to be taken to the seacoast and be made into a sleek sailing ship to sail across the Mediterranean. I would carry men and women to new adventures, and bring back the riches of Rome to our land."

The third tree lifted up its branches and said, "I want to be left alone. I want to stand here on the mountain, as straight as I can, and let my top branches reach heavenward, so that all men who see me, as they walk on the mountain road, may lift up their eyes to the skies and think of God. And in the summer's heat, they might find comfort under the shade of my arms."

Well, the axe came to the first, and it was hauled down the hill full of its high hopes. The carpenters received its lumber and began to build. Then the high hopes of being paneling in the Temple were dashed. For the tree instead was used to build a stable in the town of Bethlehem. The cows and the donkeys rubbed against the lumber, and the wind and the rain beat the boards and weathered them. Oh, the shame that the tree felt! Only an old stable!

The second tree was also chopped down. It found itself, as it had hoped, in the shipbuilder's shop. Its high hopes also vanished, for instead of becoming a vessel on the Mediterranean, it became a fishing boat on the shores of the Sea of Galilee. Its life was full of despair at being daily filled with oily, smelly fish. The shame of being so insignificant!

The third tree remained long after on the hillside, as it had hoped to do. But finally the axe bit into its trunk, and it was hauled down the hill into Jerusalem. Its high hopes were smothered when it found itself being shaped into—of all things—three crosses—the instruments of death for the common criminal. The shame! The sad reality of such a destiny!

AUTHOR UNKNOWN

Of course, we all know the rest of the story. Each one of these trees became more important than they ever dared dreamed was possible. One tree was used to build a stable—just a stable, where cattle and donkeys and pigs would live. How humiliating! Except, one night a star shone over that stable, and in that stable a girl named Mary gave birth to a little boy, who was named Jesus. No edifice in all the world has become more honored than that stable.

What about that fishing boat? To spend your life on a little sea, being used to catch fish seemed such a waste and so unimportant. Yet one day, the Son of God stepped onto that little boat, and it became the pulpit from which He spoke to the multitudes. No pulpit in any cathedral that has ever been built is more honored than that little boat became there on the Sea of Galilee.

As for the third tree, on one of its crosses Jesus breathed His last breath.

In every Christian church in the world the cross from that tree is symbolized. It has become the finest symbol of the faith of a billion people in every nation around the world.

Three ordinary trees on a hillside—but how significant they became!

Love Is One Package

Whether it be loving God, or loving other people, or loving yourself, it is important to remember that love is one package. It just cannot be divided. Here is a quotation, which I have cherished for many years, which says it very clearly:

> If you love yourself, you love everybody else as you do yourself. As long as you love another person less than you love yourself, you will not really succeed in loving yourself; but if you love all alike, including yourself, you will love them as one person and that person is both God and man. Thus he is a great and righteous person who, loving himself, loves all others equally.
>
> MEISTER JOHANNES ECKHART

Through all the experiences of my life I have observed what

Meister Eckhart says is true, " . . . loving himself, loves all others equally." You just do not separate love for self and love for others.

One of the favorite poets of all time is Walt Whitman. He said, "Whoever walks a furlong without sympathy walks to his own funeral dressed in his shroud."

I think no one has said it better than Walt Whitman does in these words, also from "The Song of Myself":

....
I am the man, I suffer'd, I was there.
The disdain and calmness of martyrs,
The mother of old, condemn'd for a witch, burnt with dry
   wood, her children gazing on,
The hounded slave that flags in the race, leans by the fence,
   blowing, cover'd with sweat,
The twinges that sting like needles his legs and neck, the
   murderous buckshot and the bullets,
All these I feel or am.

....
Agonies are one of my changes of garments,
I do not ask the wounded person how he feels, I myself
become the wounded person . . . .

....
Behold I do not give lectures or a little charity,
When I give I give myself.

Always remember: Learning to love yourself is in no sense narcissism. Admiration for yourself or fascination with yourself is not the kind of love for yourself that Jesus would have you experience. Some people never grow out of their infantile stage of development, in which the self is the object of one's love interest. Learning to love yourself is not falling in love with your own image. Narcissism literally blocks proper love for oneself and develops in the very deepest sense a self-hatred. In this state no human relationship can be fulfilled.

In his book *The Art of Loving*, Dr. Erich Fromm says:

. . . Freud speaks of self-love in psychiatric terms but,
nevertheless, his value judgment is the same as that of
Calvin. For him self-love is the same as narcissism, the
turning of the libido toward oneself. Narcissism is the
earliest stage in human development, and the person
who in later life has returned to this narcissistic stage
is incapable of love; in the extreme case he is insane.
Freud assumes that love is the manifestation of libido,
and that the libido is either turned toward others—
love; or toward oneself—self-love. Love and self-love
are thus mutually exclusive in the sense that the more
there is of one, the less there is of the other. If self-love
is bad, it follows that unselfishness is virtuous.

These questions arise: Does psychological observation
support the thesis that there is a basic contradiction
between love for oneself and love for others? Is love for
oneself the same phenomenon as selfishness, or are
they opposites? Furthermore, is the selfishness of modern man really a *concern for himself* as an individual,
with all his intellectual, emotional and sensual poten-
tialities? Has "he" not become an appendage of his
socio-economic role? *Is his selfishness identical with
self-love or is it not caused by the very lack of it?*

To go further, listen to these words from Dr. Viktor E.
Frankl taken from his book *The Doctor and the Soul.*

If it is a virtue to love my neighbor as a human being,
it must be a virtue—and not a vice—to love myself,
since I am a human being too. There is no concept of
man in which I myself am not included. A doctrine
which proclaims such exclusion proves itself to be in-
trinsically contradictory.

Selfishness and self-love, far from being identical, are
actually opposites. The selfish person does not love himself too much but too little: in fact he hates himself.
This lack of fondness and care for himself, which is only

one expression of his lack of productiveness, leaves him empty and frustrated. He is necessarily unhappy and anxiously concerned to snatch from life the satisfactions which he blocks himself from attaining. He seems to care too much for himself, but actually he only makes an unsuccessful attempt to cover up and compensate for his failure to care for his real self. Freud holds that the selfish person is narcissistic, as if he had withdrawn his love from others, and returned it toward his own person. It is true that selfish persons are incapable of loving themselves either.

I emphasize that love is one package, and it is very important to realize that the person who does not love himself is not a balanced or a happy person. His basic problem is that he focuses just on himself. He blocks God out of his life, and he blocks out all human relationships.

A "self-hater" may be a schizophrenic and cannot face himself, so he becomes somebody else in his own mind. On the other hand, the self-hater may become paranoid and not only hate himself, but believe that everybody else hates him. He may even reach the point not only of trying to destroy the person whom he imagines is against him, but also trying to destroy himself.

Love Demands Interest

The point I want to make is that self-love demands that we take an interest in other people. All around us there are timid people, waiting for a hand to reach out and bid them welcome into a fellowship. There are lonely people, waiting for a smile and word of cheer. There are children who cannot do for themselves. Gradually, as we express loving interest toward others, we feel them returning that love. And in the act of being loved, we can more properly love ourselves.

We have been told again and again, that "self-preservation

is the first law of nature." Yet, we find self-preservation in relationships. There are times when we can say with the prophet Jeremiah, "Oh that I had in the wilderness a lodging place . . . that I might leave my people, and go from them! . . . " (Jeremiah 9:2). Most of us have dreamed of having some desert-island paradise, where we could just get away from everybody and everything. However, the life of Robinson Crusoe is not the life that most of us would chose for very long. We shun loneliness. We can understand the little boy who one day said to his mother, "I wish I were two puppies so I could play with myself."

For many people, Christmas is a happy and wonderful time of the year, but for many other people, it is a sad and lonely time. To be alone or to be ignored when all around us people are receiving Christmas greetings is a burden hard to bear.

It was Mohammad, the Prophet of Islam, who said, "No one of you is a believer until he loves for his brother what he loves for himself." We know that human relationship is an essential element in living.

Here is one of the basic problems in youth today. America started out as a rural society. In that society families spent much time with each other. Today, life is much more complicated and many families just do not develop a loving relationship. The result is many suffering teenagers. I have been told that half the teenage deaths are caused by suicide. In one large city, a friend told me that there are twenty thousand alcoholics who are fourteen years old and younger. Many young people are not the carefree, happy persons that we think of young people as being. Three of the main problems young people face are: one, lack of love between their parents; two, drinking in the home by their parents; three, parents who never have time to take them anywhere.

I like the words the little girl wrote about the garbage man.

> We have the nicest garbage man,
> He empties out our garbage can;

He's just as nice as he can be,
He always stops and talks with me;
My mother doesn't like his smell,
But then, she doesn't know him well.

A garbage man, speaking a word of friendliness to a little girl, made a lot of difference to her.

The truth is, you never begin to love yourself until you begin to love others. Someone has written it this way:

It is in loving—not in being loved—
    The heart is blest;
It is in giving—not in seeking gifts—
    We find our guest.

If thou art hungry, lacking heavenly food—
    Give hope and cheer;
If thou art sad and would'st be comforted—
    Stay sorrow's tear.

Whatever be thy longing and thy need—
    That do thou give;
So shall thy soul be fed, and thou indeed
    Shalt truly live.

AUTHOR UNKNOWN

2

What Do You Think of Yourself?

One of the most penetrating questions ever asked on this earth is recorded in nearly identical words twice in the Bible

—once in the Old Testament and once in the New Testament. Here is the question: "What is man, that thou art mindful of him? and the son of man, that thou visitest him?" (Psalms 8:4; Hebrews 2:6).

The truth is that question has been on the lips of every one of us. We say it in different words; for example, "What am I that God would pay any attention to me?" or, "Why would God visit me?"

Your answer could be the most important fact about you. I like the story of the man who went to a boardinghouse and asked for a room. In an attempt to impress the landlady, he took out his wallet and showed her its contents. She responded, "Don't show me your wallet; show me your beliefs." That woman had keen discernment. What he *thought* was far more important than what he possessed.

What Is Man?

It is true of us that what we think of ourselves is of supreme significance. Here are four possible answers to the question *What is man?*

1.   Some people believe that this world just happened to be here—that a little cell of life began, and over a period of many, many centuries, man emerged. Man is an accident; he was never planned to be.

2.   There are others who believe that man is a machine, and can really do nothing about his destiny. On the other hand, some believe that the progress of civilization is inevitable, in spite of anything man might do. In the year 1912, somebody wrote these words, "Today we have no fear of war, of famine or pestilence. The advance of knowledge has safeguarded man from all these evils." However, since 1912, two world wars, nuclear explosions, and a host of other disasters have seemed to

doom that idea of man's inevitable progress upward. On the other hand, those who feel that man is a machine consider that he is doomed and can do nothing about his civilization or himself—that he will be inevitably destroyed. Either way, many believe that man is little more than an irresponsible machine.

3. Then there are those who believe that man is nothing more than a two-legged animal. He has no soul; he has only a living body. There is no future beyond this life, and the most that can be said about man is that he is the most intelligent of all the animals on the earth.

4. Finally, there are those who believe that man is God's child; made in His image; possessing a soul which God breathed into him—a soul that will live forever and forever and forever. Most of us have made our own theological beds in this last concept. We believe we are God's children, created to have fellowship with Him.

Then we ask the question "What was God's dream for us when we were created?" When our own children are born, one of the fantasies we dream about is being with them, living together, playing together, having fun together, creating things together. God is a father and God has the same dreams for each one of us.

I have children and grandchildren. We do not live in the same houses. But from time to time, I visit them in their homes. Sometimes I call them on the telephone; sometimes I write them letters. My children are on my mind, and I wish to be in communication with them. It pleases me very much when they respond to my "visitations" to them. On the other hand, it also pleases me when they come to see me. When the phone rings and one of them speaks, or when there is a letter from one of them in my mailbox, I am made happy—I long for fellowship with my children.

I am God's child, and in various ways He visits me. It exalts

me to feel that the Heavenly Father is pleased when I respond
to Him.

Fellowship

When God made us, He not only intended that we have
fellowship with Him, but also with other people. Therefore we
have His words "love God—your neighbor—as yourself."

A family from Vietnam, who were relocating in the United
States, sat in the area of the airplane where I sat. The mother
and a very small boy sat in seats behind, and the father and the
little six-year-old boy sat in the seats next to me. The father
could speak some English, and we could communicate reasonably well. The six-year-old boy could not understand anything I
tried to say to him. Finally, I reached out to shake hands, and
he reached up his little hand and took hold of my hand. Then
he looked at me and smiled in a beautiful way. Between me and
that little boy from Vietnam, I felt there was a bond of love and
friendship.

I am convinced that the greatest mandate of God for man is
that we rise to the place of harmony among all people.

Edwin Markham said it as well as anybody:

> There is a destiny that makes us brothers;
> > None goes his way alone:
> All that we send into the lives of others
> > Comes back into our own.
>
> I care not what his temples or his creeds,
> > One thing holds firm and fast—
> That into his fateful heap of days and deeds,
> > The soul of man is cast.

Where Are We Going?

As we ask the question "What do I think of myself?" I think we need to think not only of what we are now, but what we intend to be. We need to think not only of where we are, but where we are going.

Parents remember vividly that first day when a child went to school. It is one of the memorable days in the life of any family. Mothers have even been known to cry on the first day, as they leave a little one in school. Even so, we want our children to grow and to learn and to be searchers for the truth. The history of mankind is really a history of the search for knowledge. We know very little today, but we know a lot more than the caveman did. Isn't it possible that someday—maybe ten thousand years from now—maybe a million years from now—man will know and understand all mysteries? I hear people say, "God does not intend that we understand this." Frequently they are speaking of some sorrow or some problem. I reject that idea with my whole being. I believe there is no problem on this earth that is not capable of understanding. The people who say that some matters are not meant to be understood would close down every research project in the world! There is nothing on this earth that is not meant to be understood. We understand a lot today; we will continue to understand more. There is no more thrilling exercise in life than to search for truth. We keep working—looking—digging—thinking. I like the spirit of that old preacher who said, "Today we are going to unscrew the unscrutable." That is what God intends us to do.

Dreams Are They . . .

Not only do we search for truth and understanding, but we believe that we are co-creators with God. The very first verse in the Bible says, "In the beginning God created the heaven and the earth." We believe creation is a continuing process. Truly, God's dreams go beyond the mere creation of this world and even this universe. He continues to dream and, as His children, He wants us to dream with Him. Thomas Curtis Clark said it beautifully:

> Dreams are they—but they are God's dreams!
> Shall we decry them and scorn them?
> That men shall love one another,
> That white shall call black man brother.
> That greed shall pass from the marketplace,
> That lust shall yield to love for the race,
> That man shall meet with God face-to-face—
> Dreams are they all,
>   But shall we despise them—
>   God's dreams!
>
> Dreams are they to become man's dreams!
> Can we say nay as they claim us?
> That men shall cease from their hating,
> That war shall soon be abating,
> That the glory of kings and lords shall pale,
> That the pride of dominion and power shall fail,
> That the love of humanity shall prevail—
> Dreams are they all,
>   But shall we despise them—
>   God's dreams!

What do you think of yourself? You think of yourself as being God's child, having fellowship with Him, sharing in His work and dreaming His dreams.

3

Do Not Be Ashamed of Yourself

Some time ago a man was talking to me about the problems in life. Finally, he made this statement, "The main trouble with me is, I'm a phony."

My reply to him was that in some degree, in some area of life, every person is a "phony." The simplest definition of a *phony* would be "a person who seeks to appear to be something that he or she is not."

A Touch of Phoniness in Us All

Occasionally, someone will ask me where I got a doctor's degree. I always tell them that the first one I got (and the one that I was the proudest of) was given to me by a funeral director. I was the pastor of a church in a small town. I was only twenty-two years old at the time. In the local newspaper there appeared an obituary of someone from my church and in it was stated: "The funeral will be conducted by Dr. Charles L. Allen." Call it vanity—call it deception—call it whatever you please— I felt very flattered and I must say *pleased.* I even clipped the notice out of the paper and kept it. That young preacher enjoyed being called *Doctor.*

I notice that most of us enjoy being described as something more than really we are.

You will never offend a ten-year-old boy by saying to him, "You look old enough to be fourteen"; or, when a mother and daughter are shopping together in a store, for the clerk to say to the daughter, "Would your sister also like to buy a dress?" never offends the mother!

In the corridors of a hospital, a medical student is not offended by being called *Doctor*. If you ever are stopped for speeding, you never make a mistake in calling the policeman *Captain*.

Door-to-door salesmen have been known to say to the woman who answers the door, "Is your mother in?"

The truth is, in all of us there is a touch of phoniness. On the other hand, one of the greatest inspirations in life is the person *we can be* constantly calling to the person that we are. Marvelous things can happen to us—if we honestly and frankly begin to look at ourselves as we are, and also as we might become. Really, the greatest freedom people can attain is the freedom which frees us to become our true selves.

The Basic Facts About You

Whether we see any phoniness in ourselves or not, there are three basic facts about *you,* whoever you are.

First, *you are.* There are over four billion people on this earth; even so, you are one of them, and you are different from any other of them. You are an existing person.

Second, *you are becoming.* You are either becoming more— or you are becoming less. You are becoming better—or you are becoming worse. You are moving toward strength—or you are moving toward weakness. You are growing in fellowship with others—or you are becoming more and more wrapped up within yourself. You are moving toward life—or you are moving toward death. No one of us is standing still.

Third, *you have the choice of only one road, and that is the road that begins right where you are.* The only starting point for you is the person that you are right now. You can't go back one day or one year or ten years. Life moves in only one direction. It does not go backward. Let us emphasize, however, *that you can become free to be you.*

One of the most thrilling and glorious truths is the fact that each of us existed in the mind of God before he was born. As we study the universe, we realize that God had a purpose for everything He created, and it is wonderful to know that God has a purpose for every person, even you. He thought about you long before you were born. Sometimes we wonder what we are good for, but we can be sure that, in God's mind, we are good for something. Success in life is *finding that something* and giving ourselves to it.

There Is Only One of Each of Us

Every single thing on this earth has its one personal identity. There are literally billions of leaves on the trees of the world, but no two leaves are alike. No two snowflakes are ever identical, and no person is like *you*. The print of your finger is distinctive. There is something you can do, some special reason for your living; you are different from any other person who lives today, who ever lived in history, or will ever live in the future. It should lift us to a new sense of importance to realize that out of more than four billion people on this earth today, there is only one of each of us.

Once a sixth-grade teacher asked this question of the class: "What is here in the world today that was not here fifteen years ago?" She expected them to tell of some new invention or discovery.

One boy held up his hand and the teacher asked, "All right, Johnny, what is your answer?" He replied simply, "Me."

That little boy was wonderfully right. Something new came into this world when every little boy and every little girl in that class was born.

When each one of us realizes, *I am myself,* it works several wonderful marvels for us:

In the first place, *it will rid us of jealousy in our hearts.* We are jealous because we think somebody is more important than we are. But knowing that is not true, then we are free of our hates, prejudices, greed, and all the other destructive emotions that make a person miserable.

In the second place, *getting rid of your jealousies of other people, you begin to get busy on yourself.* You become the one person to whom you are entirely responsible. Your world and your life can be better, because *you* can make it so. Sure, there were failures yesterday, but when we become consumed with the idea of being ourselves, we shake off the guilts and unhappiness of yesterday's disappointments.

See a Picture of Yourself

Someone asked Thomas Edison how he accounted for his amazing inventive genius. He replied, "It is because I never think in words; I think in pictures." He pictured in his mind the objects he desired to invent. This picture took possession of him to the point that he gave himself totally to it. He would never give up. It has been said that before he invented the light bulb, he failed a thousand times; but he kept that picture of the light bulb in his mind, and one day, it began to give light.

A minister friend told me about a very unhappy woman who came to talk with him. She told him that all of her life, the one misfortune she had feared was poverty. Therefore, she saved every penny she could save. She didn't buy herself many things she desired, because she wanted to keep her money. She invested her money and finally amassed a modest fortune. Then a series of financial reverses came upon her, and she lost everything.

In telling him the story she concluded with, "Now, I am old and almost penniless, and there is nothing ahead for me. The fear I had of poverty has come upon me."

The wise minister said, "There you go again. You thought poverty; you feared poverty; you pictured poverty; and it all came to pass." He told her to get a different picture in her mind, to quit thinking about herself and begin thinking about making somebody else happy. For the first time she began to see other people. Fortunately, she met a wealthy woman who wanted a companion to go with her on a world tour. This lady said, "I would be delighted to go with you." That tour was the happiest experience in her life, and she became a caring companion of this older woman. In forgetting herself and thinking about somebody else, she found life's greatest happiness.

The problem in this idea of being ourselves comes about because no one of us *is* a single self. As some poet put it, "Within my earthly temple there's a crowd." There is our greedy self—passionate self—indifferent self—hurt or angry or callous self, but as the great Shakespeare put it in *Hamlet:* "To thine own self be true." Within every one of us is a true self.

For many years Dr. Halford Luccock was the famous professor of preaching in the Divinity School of Yale University. One of the principles he constantly taught his students was simply *to be themselves*. Then he would tell a story that illustrated what God could do with one person.

Sing the Note You Can Sing

For many summers a composer named Gioacchino Rossini would go out to some small village in Italy—one which could not afford an opera—and he would write an opera which the people of that village could perform. One summer, he auditioned all of the talent in this small village, and the only woman who could possibly be a leading lady was limited to only one good note. It was a middle B-flat. Rossini was not discouraged; he went right ahead and wrote the opera in which the leading lady had only that one note to sing. *But,* he surrounded that middle B-flat with such beautiful harmony that when she sang her one note, it was like an angel from heaven.

This is what life calls each of us to do. We each must sing the notes we can sing—then life surrounds us in such a way that the effort we make is beautiful; it is useful; it is satisfying.

4

The Problem of Finding Out the Person You Really Are

There comes to my mind a sentence that an old preacher said to me many, many years ago. It impressed me greatly, and I have never forgotten it. He said, "When God begins to speak, He always finishes the sentence." Then he added this, "There may be a thousand years between the subject and the predicate, but God finally puts down the period."

The Power to Become

It has often been said in referring to the Bible, "When God's Book was finished, He kept on talking." That means there is constantly new truth to learn. Also, we know that the creation is not something that happened once; it is something that is still happening. Likewise, it is difficult to know the person you really are, because you are not finished. In the Gospel of John, in the very first chapter and the twelfth verse, we lift up this phrase, " . . . to them gave he power to become. . . . " There is more to the verse, but that phrase says a whole lot. We are not what we might be; but by the grace of God we have the power to become that person.

Four Affirmations

Over and over we need to affirm four steps that we must take. First, *discover who we are.* Dr. Jekyll and Mr. Hyde were two personalities in the same man, and within us are both possibilities. We must decide which one we are.

Second, *every person must get acquainted with himself.* This is a process we never complete, but at least we work at it and, day by day, we know ourselves a little better.

The third step is *to deliver yourself.* When I was a boy, one of the odd jobs I did was to deliver newspapers. I did not have a very large route, and I learned the people on my route, and I knew where they wanted their paper put. I felt it was my job to deliver the paper to the place where it belonged. No person has delivered his life until that life is put *where it belongs.* A person who feels he is a misfit has a feeling of being a failure.

Fourth, *every life must be dedicated.* That is, the reason for its existence must be determined and accepted.

Somewhere I ran across a little poem that to me really says something:

> Girls whose faces are covered with paint—
> Have the advantage of girls whose faces ain't.

One's appearance makes a lot of difference, and it's important. Not only is our appearance important, it's also important to decide on certain standards of living. You can't just live. Every person must have some principles to live by. Without moral standards we become "beat."

Critical or Complimentary?

God gave us the capacity to speak, but this capacity can be either a great blessing or a great danger. We can be critical or complimentary, and in our speaking, we reveal our true selves. We can spend our time saying the world is beautiful, life is good. Somehow, it turns out that way. On the other hand, we can spend our time complaining and being critical, and our very speech drags us down. I have a little poem which I have known for years. Here it is:

There is something sort of pitiful about a man that growls—
Because the sun beats down too heavy or the wind howls;
Who never eats a meal that the cream ain't thick enough—
Or the coffee ain't been settled right, or else the meat's too
    tough.

Poor chap, he's just a victim of fate's oldest, meanest trick—
You will see by watching mules and men—
That it don't take brains—to kick.

Speaking of being critical, I was in a restaurant early one morning and I enjoyed overhearing this conversation.

A man was drinking his coffee and he said to the waitress, "This coffee is terrible. It tastes like kerosene oil; is it tea or coffee?"

The waitress replied, "If it tastes like kerosene oil, it's coffee. Our tea tastes like turpentine."

The point is, you can get in the habit of being critical, and everything you touch or taste becomes bad.

Not only am I a person who can talk, I am also a person who can think. Being able to think, I can make decisions. Being able to make decisions, gives me the power "to become," but it also gives me the power to become "undone." Who am I? A lot of it depends on what I have decided to be. It is truly wonderful when one declares, "I am a person."

5

When One Feels Not Counted

After every census taken in the United States, there are articles in the newspapers which state that literally millions of persons were overlooked. Those persons were not counted and really are not considered a part of the general population.

There are a lot of people who feel among those uncounted persons. Many people feel overlooked by life. They feel they never have been given their chance and their opportunity.

In a sense, this may be good because one of the lessons we need to learn is humility. I say "learn" it, because most people learn to "strut before they learn to stoop."

There is a story of a young man who was visiting in the home of a minister. After the visit was over, the minister showed his visitor out through a side exit. Crossing the exit was a low beam. The young man did not look carefully and bumped his head on the beam. The minister could not resist sermonizing a bit to his young friend. And so he said, "It is good for you to learn while you are young that there are many times in life when you have to stoop. In stooping, you will miss many hard bumps."

Nature has a way of reminding us that we need to walk with humility. If sometimes you feel you are not counted, it may be to your blessing.

We *Do* Count

On the other hand, we need to constantly remind ourselves that even though somebody may have overlooked us, we ourselves *count*. In the eyes of somebody we may be uncounted, but in our own thinking we count for something. There is a cause to live for; there is a goal to reach, a purpose to achieve, a service to render. The assurance of being useful brings, perhaps, life's greatest happiness.

Even though we sometimes feel we have not been counted, we not only reassure ourselves by the fact that we can count *for* something, we also reassure ourselves by the fact that we can count *on* something. The mathematician knows that he can count on the fact that two times two is four. If he doubted that for one moment, all his mathematics would come tumbling down. Blessed the person who has learned some principles in life of which he is sure and certain, and knows he can count on them.

There is tremendous power in believing something that is worth believing. One of the reasons that people slip out of life's backdoor is that they do not have any good reason for keeping on living. From time to time, it is good for a person to ask the question, "What am I really worth?"

One day a man asked me the question, "Who is the greatest president in the history of the United States?" Without a moment's hesitation I replied, "Lyndon B. Johnson." His face got red and he began to sputter, and he said some very derogatory things about Mr. Johnson. It was very evident that he did not like him. Finally he said, "Why do you say Lyndon B. Johnson was the greatest president? You did not know him." I replied, "No, sir, I really did not know Mr. Johnson. However, one day I was with a small group of people, and he walked over to me, put out his hand, and said, "Hello, Charles, I am glad to see you." I explained to this man that no other president had ever done that, and I liked a president who knew my name.

God Knows Your Name

There is something far greater than that. To me one of the greatest verses in all the Bible includes this phrase, " . . . and he calleth his own sheep by name . . . " (John 10:3). It almost makes cold chills run up and down my spine, when I think that God knows *my* name.

Many people think that no book ever written, other than the Bible, surpasses *Pilgrim's Progress.* My father must have believed that because when we were children, he read it through to us word for word. Since then, I have read it for myself, and I remember one scene especially, when Pilgrim was passing through the Valley of Humiliation. There he met a terrible character who barred his path and said to him, "Now, in this Valley of Humiliation, prepare thyself to die. For here I will spill thy soul." For some reason that phrase "spill thy soul" stuck in my mind, and I remembered it again not long ago when I heard a speaker make this statement: "One of the ways to spill a person's soul is to lead him to believe that he does not have a soul."

Maybe some people *have* been overlooked in the census of the United States, but in God's eyes there is no person who is overlooked. It always thrills my soul, when I hear that beautiful song "His Eye Is on the Sparrow, and I Know He Watches Me."

You Are Significant

I say to the people who are members of the church where I am pastor that they can always use my name as a reference, and many do. Rarely a week passes that I do not get an inquiry from some company or school asking about someone. I have a policy that I always say what I can good about the person, and let it go at that. I never say anything bad. On an application recently, there was a question which really struck me. It was, "What is the most significant fact you know about this person?"

As I kept pondering that question, the thought that hit me the hardest was: There *is* a significant fact about every person. It does something to you to realize there is a significant fact about *you*. The truth is there are *many* significant facts about you, and it is an inspiring experience to begin to list some of our own personal significant data. Each one of us would make a different list, but let us emphasize that there is something about each of us that is significant.

Being known by God and being a significant person means that you are not unloved.

I wrote a book entitled *You Are Never Alone*. I have heard from people all over the United States who have read it. "I have come to feel that there are far more people than I ever realized who feel alone and forgotten and unloved." I personally can understand some of the feelings because I, myself, live alone. I live in probably one of the wealthiest residential communities of the world, which is River Oaks in Houston, Texas. I am a member of the country club; I live in a beautiful house, which is large and spacious. I know that I could go and knock on most of the doors of any house in the River Oaks community, and I would be recognized and welcomed.

More than that, I am now in my twentieth year as pastor of a church with about twelve thousand members. Across these twenty years, I have had many happy associations with members of the church, and I feel loved and wanted by them. However, since my wife died, I have found life to be a different experience. When you are living with some person who loves you more than anybody else on this earth, it gives significance and meaning to your life that nothing else can give.

This leads me to another thought. I have three children; each of them is married, so now I have six children. In addition, I have nine grandchildren. I feel that each one of those children loves me, and I appreciate that fact very deeply. However, without taking anything away from the love of a child for a parent, it is not to be compared with the love of a parent for a child.

I say that to point out something else: We can talk about our love for God, but our love for God is *not to be compared with His love for us.* It goes far beyond the popular saying "There is Somebody up there who loves me." It means that I am not expendable. I would like to reemphasize that no person on this earth is expendable.

The Indispensable Man

We know that in a sense none of us is *indispensable,* however. When I cease being the pastor of the First United Methodist Church in Houston, another minister will be sent there, and the church will go right on just as it has for the last 140 years. This is true of all of us. Sooner or later, each one of us will die and the world will go on. However, let no one of us ever forget who our Heavenly Father is. We can know that He forever and eternally cares for us.

Somebody gave me a poem which goes like this:

Sometime, when you're feeling important!
Sometime, when your ego's in bloom;
Sometime, when you take it for granted
You're the best qualified in the room;

Sometime, when you feel that your going
Would leave an unfillable hole,
Just follow these simple instructions,
And see how it humbles your soul.

Take a bucket and fill it with water,
Put your hand in it, up to the wrist;
Pull it out; and the hole that's remaining,
Is a measure of how you'll be missed.

You may splash all you please when you enter,
You can stir up the water galore,
But stop, and you'll find in a minute,

That it looks quite the same as before.

The moral in this quaint example,
Is do just the best that you can;
And be proud of yourself, but remember,
There's no indispensable man.

AUTHOR UNKNOWN

The poem is true. *There is no indispensable man;* but as long as there is a loving God, there also is no *expendable* man.

Karl Downs

Always remember that you are a significant person. I am thinking of a man that probably no person who reads this book has ever heard of. His name was Karl Downs. He was a Methodist preacher in Oakland, California, who died of a heart attack at an early age. Several years before he died, he was asked by the Juvenile Court to take responsibility for a young man who was always getting in trouble. Karl Downs accepted that responsibility, and in a very kind, loving way became a substitute father for that boy. I say you have never heard of Karl Downs, but you have heard of that boy. His name was Jackie Robinson. All of us who like baseball will never forget the tremendous contribution made by the first black man to ever play major-league baseball. But had it not been for Karl Downs! He *was* a significant person. *I* am a significant person; *you* are a significant person; *everybody* is significant.

6

Take the Responsibility for Yourself

There is a verse in the Bible which begins like this, "A man should thoroughly examine himself . . . (1 Corinthians 11:28 PHILLIPS). A few weeks ago I had what was described to me as bronchitis. I bought some cough medicine at the drugstore and took it, but it did not seem to help me. After about a week, I went to see my physician. He explained to me that I should have come to see him a week ago. But we have a tendency to put off calling the doctor as long as we can. He checked on my bronchitis and gave me a prescription. Then he said, "Since you are here, I need to give you an examination." He proceeded to do just that. He took samples of my blood, X-rayed me, listened to my chest, and did all the things that doctors do in examining a person.

We all know that a regular examination by a physician is good. In yet another way, a person needs to examine himself. Sometimes when we do examine ourselves, we are tempted to obscure what we see through rationalization. An insurance adjuster estimated that upwards of 90 percent of the people involved in automobile accidents see themselves as blameless. It is also hard for a person to admit that he is an alcoholic; and sometimes we hear the phrase, "I do not mean to be gossiping, but did you hear . . . ?" Illicit sex affairs can become in our minds "expressions of love." This is rationalization.

A psychologist visited a penitentiary and began asking prisoners, "Why are you here?" The answers were interesting, even though they were expected. There were lots of them, "I was framed." "They ganged up on me." "It was a case of mistaken identity. It was not me—it was somebody else." The psychologist concluded that you cannot find a larger group of innocent people than in a prison!

It is so easy to rationalize our behavior when we look at ourselves. But every so often, we need to say with the Psalmist:

> Search me, O God, and know my heart: try me, and know my thoughts: And see if there be any wicked way in me, and lead me in the way everlasting.
>
> Psalms 139:23, 24

Somewhere I read that Lady Montague wrote her daughter, "It is eleven years since I have seen my face or figure in a glass. The last reflection I saw there was so disagreeable that I resolved to spare myself such mortification in the future." Many of us understand and empathize with Lady Montague. We look at our faces in the glass, but we refuse to look at our lives. That is because what we see there requires tremendous adjustments that we do not want to make.

Let us hammer home the point that all of us need to be responsible for ourselves. One of the thrilling experiences in reading the Bible is that oftentimes you suddenly see a new truth in something that you had read many times. Several years ago, I was reading in chapter sixteen, verse thirteen of Matthew's Gospel that Jesus said to His disciples, "Whom do men say that I the Son of man am?" They were very quick with the replies. There were a lot of opinions on the street about Jesus, and it's easy to quote what people are saying.

Then suddenly Jesus looked straight at them and said, "But whom say ye that I am?" (v. 15). That is a different question altogether. It's one thing to talk about the opinions of others; it is something else to talk about what *you* believe. As I read that, suddenly it dawned upon me that I had grown up in the church, and that all through my life I had never had reason to question the basic beliefs that I had been taught. I said to myself, *Regardless of what my father believed or what other people have told me, what do I believe?* The question would not leave me, and I kept thinking—not about what I ought to believe, not what I had been told to believe, but, literally, *what do I believe?* I could not get away from it, so I put down what I believed and it was published in an autobiography, *What I Have Lived By.*

The point is, you are not responsible for what somebody else believes. *The important question is:* "Whom do you say that I am?"

To me, this seems to define what it really means to come of age—to become a responsible self. We grow up when we reach the point at which we can give answers for ourselves.

Two Questions

Across the years, I have spent many, many hours in counseling with people. My method is to ask two questions and be quiet. The first question is "What is your situation?" I listen carefully as the person tells me the story. Then my second question is "What do you intend to do about it?" And most of the time, I get a perfectly good answer. The business of a counselor is to help a person to face up to his situation, and then give an answer for it.

In order to become responsible for ourselves, first we need to be honest. When the doctor took an X ray of my chest recently, he would honestly say what he saw if anything were wrong. He took a cardiogram. Had there been a problem, he would have told me so. Not so when we are examining ourselves! It is so easy to see a problem and then excuse it. How many times have such statements as these been made: "I was not loved when I was a child"; "my schoolteachers were not capable"; "my parents were too strict"; "we married too young"; "my boss has it in for me"; "I have been cheated" and so on and so on! The point is, it is easy to excuse problems rather than solve them.

Your Own Policeman

Across the years, one of the ministers who inspired me the most was Dr. Pierce Harris, who for twenty-five years was pastor of First Methodist Church in Atlanta, Georgia. He and I used to preach together, and play golf together, and from him I learned a lot. One of the expressions he used to use was "Every man is his own policeman." And then he would frequently quote the familiar words of Shakespeare from *Hamlet:*

> To thine own self be true,
> And it must follow, as the night the day,
> Thou canst not then be false to any man.

We need to realize that in a sense life is personal and individual: *to thine own self.* Once a man told me that he had a detective follow his wife, because he wanted to maintain and protect his home. I told him that he did not have a home; he had nothing to protect, because he had surrendered love and confidence and that which makes a home. A home is in your heart and, if you have to hire a detective, you do not have a home. When it comes to your home, you need to be your own policeman. To "police yourself" means to take custody and to be responsible for your safety. It also means to arrest yourself when you are in the wrong.

It's interesting to be driving along the highway and see a police car. Immediately, all the cars along the highway slow down. If we policed ourselves, then we would not be worried about the police cars on the highway.

Actually, a policeman is to protect the safety of the public, and when you become your own policeman, what you are doing is protecting your own life. "To thine own self be true"—that is, be responsible for protecting your own best interests.

Our Money

There are several areas where we need to police ourselves. One of the first places I mention is the need to police our own pocketbooks. Money problems cause probably more unhappiness than any other area. I frequently say to couples whom I marry that they need to get the money question settled. There are many ways to handle your money, but no couple can be happy together until they agree on the money question. I have worked with more couples than I can count over the problems they have gotten into because of credit. They get credit cards, and it is so easy to buy any and everything they want. Then they reach the point at which they realize that their payments are more than their income. Young couples have a tendency of wanting to start off on the level of their parents, forgetting the fact that their parents have worked up to that position over a period of many years.

My wife and I married when I was a student in the seminary. After I graduated, I received the appointment to be the pastor of several little mountain churches. This was back in the Depression, and nobody had any money. My salary was very low. However, I had to have a car, and so we bought a car on the installment plan. Paying for that car is where I got my idea of eternity! Then came the day when I mailed the last check, and the car was paid for. I will never forget how we sat down together, and we made two resolutions. First, from that day on, *we would never buy anything on credit.* We never broke that resolution. What we were thinking about primarily were items that people eat up or wear out.

If a couple buys a house, for example, that is an investment, and I do not count that. However, I would never buy furniture to put in the house, until I could pay for it. Not long ago I visited in the home of a young couple. The dining room was completely empty. I commented on the fact, and the girl said, "Take a look in our bedroom." I looked, and there on the floor was a large piece of foam rubber. They did not have bedroom furniture,

either. She explained to me that they wanted that house, and
they could meet the payments. At that point, however, they did
not feel they could meet furniture payments. Therefore they
were doing without furniture until the time they could afford
it.

It is amazing what people can do without if they are only
willing to; and there are a lot of things I would do without
rather than be in debt for.

The other resolution my wife and I made was that a tithe of
all the church paid us we would give back. That we have also
kept, and today I can testify that you cannot outgive God. God
takes great joy in giving.

Of course, this works both ways. To be the policeman of your
pocketbook doesn't mean just to keep from spending. I said to
a friend of mine the other day, "What's the use of being the
richest man in the cemetery?" I could have quoted him the
words of Jesus, "For what shall it profit a man, if he shall gain
the whole world, and lose his own soul?" (Mark 8:36). Here is
a man who thinks success in life is determined by how much
you reach out and grab hold of, and then hang on to.

Our Hearts

However, let's climb a little higher in the area of living. The
Bible says, "Keep thy heart with all diligence . . . " (Proverbs
4:23).

When I use the word *heart,* I am not talking about that
physical organ in the body. It is important to exercise, eat the
proper food, and not do the things that would bring on a heart
attack. However, when the Bible speaks of "keep thy heart," it
isn't the *physical* organ, but rather it is that spirit within you
where God speaks. Your heart is where the soft winds of sympathy blow; your heart is where friendliness blooms; your heart
is where the laugh of love is heard. Your heart is your spirit and
your attitude. We need to be policemen of our hearts. Such sins
as envy and jealousy, malice and prejudice can get inside of our

hearts and make them cold and hard. Grudges can be held in our hearts. Life is just too short to hold an unforgiving spirit.

Here we might say just a word about marriage. Most of the human problems today are in reference to marriage. Read carefully this verse:

We marvel at the silence that divides the living and the dead.
Yet more apart
Are those who all life long live side-by-side
Yet never heart by heart.

AUTHOR UNKNOWN

If marriage is to be what we want it to be, and what God intended it to be, it must be "heart by heart."

There is another area in which we need to be policemen of our hearts. We use the expression "Don't lose heart." Discouragement involves our hearts—giving up and quitting. Many, many people have lost out in life because they "lost heart." When you feel like quitting, that is the time when you need to take over as your own policeman.

To me one of the most beautiful and inspiring passages in all of literature comes from Ernest Hemingway's wonderful story "A Natural History of the Dead." In it he said:

When that persevering traveller, Mungo Park, was at one period of his course fainting in the vast wilderness of an African desert, naked and alone, considering his days as numbered and nothing appearing to remain for him to do but lie down and die, a small moss-flower of extraordinary beauty caught his eye. "Though the whole plant," says he, "was no larger than one of my fingers, I could not contemplate the delicate confirmation of its roots, leaves and capsules without admiration. Can that Being who planted, watered and brought to perfection, in this obscure part of the world, a thing which appears of so small importance, look with uncon-

cern upon the situation and suffering of creatures
formed after his own image? Surely not. Reflections
like these would not allow me to despair; I started up
and, disregarding both hunger and fatigue, travelled
forward, assured that relief was at hand; and I was not
disappointed."

In that beautiful story one little tiny flower kept a fainting,
naked wanderer in the wilderness from giving up and quitting.

Our Minds

There is a third area in which all of us must be our own
policemen, and that is of our minds. In probably the last letter
he wrote, Paul said to his young friend, Timothy, "For God hath
not given us the spirit of fear; but of power, and of love, and of
a sound mind" (2 Timothy 1:7). And writing to the Romans,
Paul said, " . . . be ye transformed by the renewing of your
mind . . . " (Romans 12:2).

For a long time we have known that man's failures and his
successes are the direct results of his thoughts. Weakness and
strengths, purity and impurity are brought about by the way
we think. Sadness and happiness come from inside our own
minds. We achieve, we conquer, we make progress by changing
our thoughts. On the other hand, we remain weaklings and
miserable by refusing to change our thoughts. We may be
greedy, dishonest, vicious, but on the other hand, we may be
honest, loving, virtuous—it all depends on the way we think.

The search for knowledge is a mental process. Spiritual
achievement comes through holy aspirations, which are the
result of noble and lofty thoughts.

One of the books considered today a true classic is entitled,
As a Man Thinketh by James Allen. In that book he says:

A man's mind may be likened to a garden, which may
be intelligently cultivated or allowed to run wild; but

whether cultivated or neglected, it must, and will, *bring forth*. . . .

Just as a gardener cultivates his plot, keeping it free from weeds, and growing the flowers and fruits which he requires, so may a man tend the garden of his mind, weeding out all the wrong, useless, and impure thoughts, and cultivating toward perfection the flowers and fruits of right, useful, and pure thoughts. By pursuing this process, a man sooner or later discovers that he is the master-gardener of his soul, the director of his life. He also reveals, within himself, the laws of thought, and understands, with ever-increasing accuracy, how the thought-forces and mind-elements operate in the shaping of his character, circumstances, and destiny.

I know of no person who has said it better.

The point is, we are determined by the way we think. Outside circumstances can neither make us nor destroy us. The failures are usually due to inner weaknesses, rather than to outer pressures. When we permit worries and fears and anxieties and doubts to possess our minds, eventually we are going to be defeated.

In the novel *Gone With the Wind*, at the funeral of Gerald O'Hara, his prospective son-in-law gives the eulogy. He says:

. . . There warn't nothin' that come to him *from the outside* that could lick him.

He warn't scared of the English government when they wanted to hang him. He just lit out and left home. And when he come to this country and was pore, that didn't scare him a mite neither. He went to work and he made his money. And he warn't scared to tackle this section when it was part wild and the Injuns had just been run out of it. He made a big plantation out of a wilderness. And when the war come on and his money begun to go, he warn't scared to be pore again. And when the Yan-

kees came through Tara and might of burnt him out or
killed him, he warn't fazed a bit and he warn't licked
neither. He just planted his front feet and stood his
ground. That's why I say he had our good points. There
ain't nuthin' *from the outside* can lick any of us.

But he had our failin's too, cause he could be licked
from the inside. I mean to say that what the whole
world couldn't do, his own heart could. . . .

All you all and me, too, are like him. We got the same
weakness and failin'. There ain't nothin' that walks
can lick us, any more than it could lick him, not Yan-
kees nor Carpetbaggers nor hard times nor high taxes
nor even downright starvation. But that weakness
that's in our hearts can lick us in the time it takes to
bat your eye. . . .

MARGARET MITCHELL

We do not have to be "licked from the inside." The Psalmist
gave us the answer and we can depend on it: "I sought the Lord,
and he heard me, and delivered me from all my fears" (34:4).

As policemen of our minds, let us stand on guard to keep
thoughts out of our thinking that ought not to be there—to
admit those which are uplifting and inspiring. We *can* control
our own thinking.

Our Tongues

There are other areas in life where we need to be our own
policemen. Let me mention one other. We need to police our
tongues. Every so often, we need to read the words of James,
"If any man among you seem to be religious, and bridleth not
his tongue, but deceiveth his own heart, this man's religion is
vain" (James 1:26).

Immediately there comes to mind the area of profanity.
Many people get into the habit of using profane words. For
example, take the word *hell.* We hear people constantly com-

pare things to hell, such as, "It is cold as hell"; "it is hot as hell"; "that car was going as fast as hell," and so on. I have never seen why so many people want to use *hell* as a point of comparison. However, the other day, a man came into my office and I really think he used it correctly. He said to me, "Preacher, I am in a hell of a shape."

Profane words have a tendency to level out the high peaks of our souls. However, I am inclined to believe that much of our so-called profanity is more silly than sinful. To me the most profane word in the English language is the word *hopeless*. The Psalmist said, " . . . hope thou in God . . . " (Psalms 42:5). The word *hopeless* is profane because it denies the existence of God. As long as we believe in God, we are *never* hopeless. When we become hopeless, we surrender, we quit, we lose heart, we fail. *Hopeless* is profane because it destroys the very best endeavors, even the very best person. Police your tongue—never let the word *hopeless* cross your lips.

The theme of this entire book is *Love God—love your neighbor—love yourself.* When you learn to love yourself, you never want to hurt your neighbor.

There is a legend which has been often repeated, but it does not hurt us to read it again. The legend tells of one with a troubled conscience, who went to the village priest for advice. He had repeated some slander about a friend and later had found that his words were untrue. He asked the priest what he could do to make amends. The priest told the man: "If you want to make peace with your conscience, you must fill a bag with goose feathers, and go to every door in the village, and drop a feather on each porch."

The peasant took a bag, filled it with goose feathers, and did as he was told. Then he went back to the priest and asked, "Is this all that I need to do?"

"No, that is *not* all," was the answer. "There is one thing more: take your bag and gather up every feather."

The peasant left. After a long period he returned, saying, "I could not find all the feathers, for the wind had blown them away."

The priest said, "So it is with gossip. Unkind words are so easily dropped, but we can never take them back again."

Let that story stick in your mind, and whenever you are tempted to say an unkind word, remembering the feathers, you will hesitate. The truth is many of us talk when we ought to be quiet.

I have a story which I have enjoyed for many years. I think one of the reasons I like the story so well is because I have enjoyed the humor of the three persons involved. According to the story, ventriloquist Edgar Bergen, Jack Benny, and George Burns went to a restaurant for dinner. When they finished, Jack Benny said to the waiter, "I will take the check." The waiter handed Jack the check, and he paid it.

On the way out, George Burns said to Jack Benny, "It surely was nice of you to ask for the check."

Jack replied, "I did not ask for the check, and that is the last time I will ever have dinner with a ventriloquist."

The point of the story is that we should do our own talking and not let somebody else speak for us.

Many years ago I memorized what is called "A Short Course in Human Relations." Here it is:

The 6 most important words:
I admit I made a mistake.
The 5 most important words:
You did a good job.
The 4 most important words:
What is your opinion?
The 3 most important words:
If you please.
The 2 most important words:
Thank you.
The *1* most important word:
We.
The least important word:
I.

There is one other point that needs to be mentioned, and that is that gossip never does any harm—until someone makes an issue out of it. Gossip is both nasty and sickly, but will die if it is left alone.

7

Personal Power Comes From a Purpose

The great Leonardo da Vinci said it this way, "Iron rusts from disuse, stagnant water loses its purity, and in cold weather becomes frozen; even so does inaction sap the vigors of the mind."

Inaction also lowers one opinion of oneself.

When I think about purpose, three scenes in the Bible come to my mind. The first one is this:

> . . . when the time was come that he should be received up, he stedfastly set his face to go to Jerusalem.
>
> LUKE 9:51

Underscore the word *stedfast*. Jesus' eyes were fixed on a goal —dedicated to a purpose—committed to a principle. Even if death stood between Him and that purpose, He would not be

shaken from it. It was this purpose that gave Him the power
to go through Gethsemane and up a hill called Calvary.

Next, I turn back to the Old Testament to the Book of Nehemiah. The walls of Jericho had been torn down; the people were
discouraged, the enemies were all around. The prophet set
about the task of rebuilding the wall. His own people ridiculed
him; every obstacle was thrown in his way. Four times the
demand was given for him to give up the task, and four times
his answer was " . . . I am doing a great work, so that I cannot
come down . . . " (Nehemiah 6:3).

Now look at one more scene. Simon Peter is preaching on the
day of Pentecost. He and the others had been in the Upper
Room where the Spirit power of God had come upon their lives.
He says to the people, " . . . Save yourselves from this untoward generation" (Acts 2:40).

Look at that word *untoward*. It is not a word that is used in
our modern language. It is used only this *one* time in the Bible.
However, it is a good word; it means "not going toward anything—running around in circles—no specific direction—no
purpose." *Untoward* means a meaningless existence.

There we have it: *stedfastly set his face—I am doing a great
work—untoward.*

If our lives are to be dominated by some great purpose, there
are three things we must know.

Life Is a Journey

First, *life is a journey.*

In the eighteenth century there lived a philosopher by the
name of Gotthold Ephraim Lessing. He spoke well and wisely
when he said:

> If God should hold enclosed in his right hand all truth,
> and in his left hand only the ever-active impulse after
> truth, although with the condition that I must always
> and forever err, I would with humility turn to his left

hand and say, "Father, give me this: pure truth is for thee alone."

We cherish the words of our founding fathers of this nation when they talked about "life, liberty, and the pursuit of happiness." The words *pursuit* and *purpose* must go together. If you possess pursuit without purpose, you become *untoward*—you start going around in circles—not getting anywhere.

Every stream of water in the world—a branch, a creek, a river—has one purpose. The purpose of every stream in this earth is to flow toward the sea. When the stream stops that pursuit, it becomes a swamp. Likewise, when a life loses its purpose and stops its pursuit, it becomes stagnated and stalemated. When life ceases to be a journey, it becomes an unhappy burden.

I have known many people who lost respect for themselves; some even began to hate themselves, because they felt they had lost their reason for living.

Keep Going

In the second place, because life is a journey, *we must keep going.* "He stedfastly set his face." He kept His eyes on the purpose, and He was ever moving toward that goal.

Jesus once said, "No man, having put his hand to the plow, and looking back, is fit for the kingdom of God." (Luke 9:62).

A purpose in life keeps us going. It will put us back on our feet when we have been knocked down.

Sometimes we do wrong, and then we feel guilt, remorse, and shame. Feeling guilt is worth nothing—unless it leads to change. Many people give their sins a "prolonged funeral." That is, they spend themselves in their past mistakes and are never able to recapture the high purposes of their lives.

The great psychologist William James said it this way: "Repentance is not grovelling over sins committed, but a rising and shaking one's self free from the guilty feelings and turning to that which is good."

Considered one of the great stories in the Bible is the twelfth chapter of 2 Samuel. David's son was very sick. David constantly was praying for the child. Not only that, he refused to eat, and he would lie on the ground all night, praying for that child. After seven days the boy died. David then got up and washed his face, changed his clothes, came into the house, worshiped, and then sat down at the table and began to eat.

As long as the child was sick, the thought of his getting well consumed all of David's life. But when the child died, he felt it was time to get up and get going again.

Here on this earth we come to love each other more than we love ourselves, and then we become separated through what we call death. It never is easy, but we need to keep going. Occasionally I say to some person, "You can hold a person in your love, but you cannot stay married to a dead person." You never turn loose of the precious memories, but life must go on. I like these words:

> Build on resolve, and not upon regret,
> The structure of thy future . . .
> Waste no tears upon the blotted record of lost years
> But turn the leaf, and smile . . . Oh, smile, to see
> The fair white pages that remain for thee.
>
> AUTHOR UNKNOWN

Do Not Be Discouraged

In the third place, *do not be discouraged because you have not yet achieved your purposes.* Many of us like football. The purpose in football is to score a touchdown. Sometimes a touchdown might be scored in just one play. A player may take a kickoff and run the entire length of the field; or a pass play may go for, say, eighty yards. However, in football, you just have to go ten yards to make a first down, and a team does not have to go ten yards in one play. A team has four plays to make a first down, so a team can only make three yards or four yards on a play, and still eventually cross that goal line.

I have a friend who told me that once when he was in New York City, he had to walk eighty blocks. He did not have money for transporation. At first he said to himself, "I cannot walk eighty blocks." But he kept thinking about it, and he decided that he only had to walk one block at a time. He realized that by walking *one block at a time,* eventually, he could walk the eighty blocks.

ONE STEP AT A TIME

One step at a time, that's all it takes
    to walk the longest road.
One step at a time, that's all you need
    to carry the biggest load.

One step at a time, and the desert waste
    is finally left behind;
The top of the mountain comes into view,
    or your rainbow's gold you find.

One step at a time is all God asks
    on the highway of the soul;
Till you look and see, just a prayer away,
    your faith-appointed goal!

WINIFRED BRAND

We need to remind ourselves that this principle is true in all of our living. This idea of living one day at a time is a sound principle. We have not reached our goals, and let us be thankful that that is true. Let us remind ourselves that life is a pursuit and not necessarily the accomplishment.

A Five-Year Plan

I knew of an outstanding lady who ran a home for retired people. She found that many of these people sat around this home bored, doing nothing, and really missing all of the joys of life. She worked out what she called a "five-year plan." She would talk to each one of the people about setting a goal that could be reached in five years. She had wonderful results. One lady said that she had always wanted to paint, and as a result of the five-year plan, she took painting lessons and literally accomplished her dream. A man revealed that his lifelong goal had been to read the New Testament in Greek. She got in touch with a Greek teacher for him and long before the five years were up, he had literally read the New Testament in Greek.

This wonderful woman also convinced the residents that you do not have to accomplish all of life's purpose in one effort. To be a successful person means that you have been saved from a scattered, meaningless life.

Through the years, I have been inspired by the story of Glenn Cunningham. He was born on a Kansas farm and attended a one-room school. He and his brother had the job of making the fire at the school every morning. One morning they poured kerosene on live coals of fire, and the stove exploded. Glenn hurried to the door, but then he realized that his brother was not with him. He turned and went back for his brother, and they were both badly burned. His brother died, and Glenn's legs were burned severely. Long before that accident, Glenn Cunningham had dreamed of breaking the world's record in running a mile. He was deeply disappointed. He felt for a period that all of the reasons for his existence were gone, but, gradually, he learned to walk again and even began to run; but it was a slow, painful process. At twenty-five years of age, he could not walk very well. However, he went on to break the world's record for the one-mile run.

In spite of what happened, Glenn Cunningham held on to his purpose and his purpose made him walk again—his purpose made him run again—his purpose gave him reasons for living and, eventually, self-respect. Because of his purpose Cunningham kept believing in himself.

8
Learn to Believe, Dream, and Ask

You see things; and you say why?
> *but I dream of things that never were*
> *and I say why not. . . .*
> GEORGE BERNARD SHAW

Many people were deeply inspired in reading Dag Hammarskjold's private diary, which was published after his death. There was one statement he made which especially inspired me. He said, "I don't know WHO—or WHAT—put the question. I don't even know when it was put. I don't even remember answering, but at some moment I did answer YES to SOMEONE or SOMETHING—and from that hour I was certain that existence is meaningful, and that therefore my life has a goal."

There are in every person marvelous possibilities—if he will just believe, commit himself, and work at it. I am thinking now about a man who was born in a simple, rural community. He had few of the opportunities of life, little chance to go to school, and the material possessions of his family were meager. As a little boy, he dreamed of being a preacher, and often he would stand in a chair and preach to an imaginary congregation. He had a natural gift for singing, and though he never had opportunity to study music, he became a member of the choir in a monastery. As a young man he joined the church.

A Multitalented Boy

He had a good mind, and when he was eleven years old, he made all *A's* in school, and the other pupils naturally looked up to him as their leader. One of the things he enjoyed was reading the books of James Fenimore Cooper about Indians and cowboys, and he delighted to act out those marvelous stories.

He loved great music, and it is said that he heard Wagner's *Lohengrin* ten times in succession. He reached the point where he could whistle long passages from operas and would entertain his friends. He became a reader of history and philosophy; in art and architecture he also found unusual interest.

A tragedy came into his life when he was fourteen years old. His father died, and he became the "man of the family." When he was seventeen years old, he went to live in a city. He had a small inheritance, which he had received from his father, so he had time to visit art museums, attend opera, read, and think. Whenever he was with a group of friends, he always was the center of attention because of his ability to impersonate great characters.

He had only been in the city one year, when his mother became seriously ill. He hurried home and devoted himself entirely to caring for her. When she died, he was grief stricken for many weeks and even months. He would not accept the inheritance his mother left him, so he gave it to a sister. To another sister he gave an inheritance from an aunt.

Later, his country declared war on some other countries, and he volunteered for the army. He was a good soldier, and he was decorated for bravery.

A Man Who Loved

While he was in the army, a little dog ran into the trench, where he was waiting. He caught the little dog, began to pet it and feed it, and they made friends with each other. Later someone stole the little dog, and for days this man was almost beside himself with grief.

Once he found some hungry mice, and he would regularly feed them crumbs of bread. He seemed not to want to hurt anything or anybody.

He especially loved people who had never had an opportunity in life. Once a poor man gave him two eggs, and he was deeply moved with gratitude. He loved children and he would make colorful and beautiful kites for the youngsters of the community. One day a little boy bumped his head against a chair and began to cry. To show his loving sympathy, this man beat his own head against the chair. Then for the sake of the little boy, he spanked the chair.

When he got out of the army, he was twenty-nine years old. He wanted to serve his nation in some way. He seemed to have no personal ambitions—he just wanted to give and help people. When he was thirty-four years old, he wrote a beautiful poem about his mother, in which he pleaded with people to love their own mothers.

Who Was This Man?

Then we ask the question: Who was this man? We are really surprised when we learn that his name was Adolph Hitler. I think we would all agree that he became probably the most destructive and diabolical personality in all of history. This man, who loved people, ended up by killing millions and bringing untold suffering.

Every person has an equal capacity for good or for evil. The greatest saint has the ability to be the most evil, and the most evil person has the ability to be the most saintly. Whatever our inner capacity is, it can go in either direction.

Life's Six Great Moments

As we study life, we find that life really revolves around six great moments.

First, *there is the moment of birth.* We did not choose when we were born, or where we were born, or who our parents were. This we had no control over. On the other hand, we are not bound by the circumstances of birth. Perhaps we would prefer to have been born with the proverbial "silver spoon in our mouths." Perhaps we look with envy toward those who are born with a prestigious name, with wealth, and with all the opportunities of life. But, we also remember a Baby was born in a stable and became the Saviour of the world. Another baby was born in a small cabin, and Abraham Lincoln became president. History is replete with the stories of men and women who overcame defeating circumstances of birth.

The second great moment in your life is *when you realize that someone loves you and cares for you.* Fortunately, for most of us that comes at the very beginning of life. One generation ago, when a baby was born in a hospital, the mother would stay ten to twelve days. The only time the baby was brought to be with the mother was at feeding time. Now that is changed. The mother does not stay in the hospital but three or four days to begin with, and in many hospitals, the baby is allowed to stay a lot more time in the bed with the mother. Even in the first week of life, infants can begin to realize that somebody loves and cares for them. Certainly to be pitied is the child who grows up without love.

The third moment is *when you realize that there is a God who knows you, who forgives you, and has a purpose for your life.*

The fourth great moment is *when you decide what you intend to do with your life.* I am not thinking here so much of the particular job or profession; I am thinking of whether you decide to live a life of self or a life of service.

The fifth great moment in your life is *when you get married.* Marriage is a marvelous, wonderful experience.

Then, finally, the sixth great moment of your life, is *when you die.*

Dreams Have No Limit

Just now, in these pages, we are particularly concerned with that moment of deciding what you intend to do with your life. We need to remember that our dreams are more important than the cars we drive. A car depreciates very quickly, but noble dreams have no limit. When we stop dreaming, we really stop living.

Recently a friend of mine sent me the following poem. I have read it and reread it, and I think it is wonderful.

KEEPING ON

I've dreamed many dreams that never came true,
I've seen them vanish at dawn;
But I've realized enough of my dreams, thank God,
To make me want to dream on.

I've prayed many prayers when no answer came,
I've waited patient and long;
But answers have come to enough of my prayers
To make me keep praying on.

I've trusted many a friend who failed
And left me to weep alone;
But I've found enough of my friends true-blue
To make me keep trusting on.

I've sown many seeds that fell by the way
For the birds to feed upon;

But I've held enough golden sheaves in my hand,
To make me keep sowing on.

I've drained the cup of disappointment and pain,
I've gone many days without song,
But I've sipped enough nectar from the rose of life
To make me want to live on.

AUTHOR UNKNOWN

When we begin to *believe* that we can do them, marvels can be accomplished. The trouble is that we give up before we get started.

9

Do Not Be Afraid to Ask

If you believe in the first place, you are willing to ask. Many years ago, I heard a story about a six-year-old boy. In the little town where he lived, there was a store giving away caps to little boys. They were Pillsbury Best Flour caps. I can remember those caps when I was a child. Any boy who wanted one could go into the store, ask for it, and get it. He watched other youngsters go in and come out proudly, each wearing one of those caps.

Finally, he got up enough nerve to go in. He saw there was only one cap left; then he lost his nerve, and without saying a word, turned, and walked out.

One of his friends said to him, "Did you get the cap?"

He replied, "No, I didn't want one."

That boy's name was Douglas E. Lurton, who grew up to become an outstanding reporter and a writer of wonderful books. He later said that every time he thought of that story, he felt like crying. However, as a writer and a student of people, he later came to the conclusion that most of the time people win or lose the things they want by simply asking for them or *not* asking for them.

This is certainly in line with the teachings of Jesus Christ.

It's in the Scriptures

Here are several references from the New Testament. We are familiar with each one of these, but reading them over will reemphasize their importance:

- Ask, and it shall be given you . . . For every one that asketh receiveth. . . .

  MATTHEW 7:7, 8

- Again I say unto you, That if two of you shall agree on earth as touching any thing that they shall ask, it shall be done for them of my Father which is in heaven.

  MATTHEW 18:19

- And whatsoever ye shall ask in my name, that will I do, that the Father may be glorified in the Son.

  JOHN 14:13

- If ye abide in me, and my words abide in you, ye shall ask what ye will, and it shall be done unto you.

  JOHN 15:7

- If any of you lack wisdom, let him ask of God . . . and it shall be given him.

  JAMES 1:5

There are many other verses from the Bible that could be quoted in reference to asking, but really James summed it all up when he said, " . . . ye have not, because ye ask not" (James 4:2).

When you do not believe then you begin to be negative, saying, "I cannot do that," or, "That is too good for me to hope for," or, "There is no reason for me to try," and on and on. There is no way of measuring what we miss because we never learn to believe, and, not believing, we never ask.

Here let me be very personal. There is no way for me to express the admiration that I hold for my mother and my father. Neither of them had the opportunity to go to school that they would have liked to have had. My father spent a total of three months in a little college and that was it. He was almost thirty years old when he entered the ministry, and he served more than forty years as the minister in very small towns. His salary was always meager. In fact, when he died, he had a total of two hundred dollars.

Fourteen Degrees

There were seven children in our family. None of us can explain how our parents did it, but they sent all seven of us through college. In fact, we received fourteen college degrees among us! They gave us what little money they had, but they gave us a lot of inspiration, and they made us believe that we could do it.

I finished Young Harris College, a small but wonderful junior college in north Georgia. I wanted to go on to college, but my brother John finished high school that year, and there was absolutely no way that my mother and father could help both of us. Since I had already been to college two years, it was John's turn to go.

All that summer I tried to get a job, but the only job I could get was playing baseball, and that did not pay very much. I saved a few dollars—but just a few. Along about the middle of August, I was facing a pretty dismal winter. I had no job and nowhere to go.

Somebody told me about Wofford College. I had never heard of Wofford College, but I made inquiry and found that it was a

Methodist college in Spartanburg, South Carolina. I wrote a letter to the president of Wofford College, although I did not even know his name. I explained to him that I had no money, but I wanted to continue in college. By return mail I received a letter from Dr. Henry Nelson Snyder, the president of Wofford College. He opened the door for me to come there. School was to begin in just a week. My mother washed and patched what clothes I had. We put them in an old suitcase, and I got on the bus and headed for Spartanburg, South Carolina.

As I write these words, I am remembering that just a month ago, I was preaching in Lake Junaluska, North Carolina. In the congregation I saw Dr. C. C. Norton, who now lives there. He was one of my professors at Wofford. I remember him especially, because he was the one who nominated me for Phi Beta Kappa, and through these years, I have cherished that scholastic honor.

The point is, I never would have gone to Wofford College *if I had not asked.*

I mentioned earlier that one of the six greatest moments in your life is getting married. It is an interesting experience to be in a group of couples and ask the question, "How did you meet your wife or your husband?" You get all kinds of answers. I like to tell my own story.

I never will forget the day I walked into the chapel at Young Harris College. I saw a girl sitting on the stage, playing a violin. I did not know who she was, where she was from, or anything about her. But as I saw that girl, I said, "That is the girl I am going to marry."

The next day I was in a group where she was. I walked over to her and said, "Will you marry me?"

She replied, "Yes."

Then my next question was, "What is your name?"

That is a true story. We did marry (after a four-year courtship), and "lived happily ever-afterward."

The point is, I got my wife because I had the nerve to ask her!

Four Principles in Asking

1. *Decide what you really want.* God gave to us the marvelous ability called *imagination.* Actually, it is like having a motion-picture screen in your mind. You can put on that screen a picture and look at it. When you are thinking of your own life, keep putting on the screen of your mind the picture of what you really want. Put it on, take it off, put it on, take it off. Keep working at it, until that picture is clearly focused on the screen of your mind.

    Then test that picture with such questions as: *Is it good for you? Is it fair to all others concerned? Are you ready for it now? Do you honestly feel it is according to God's will?* When that mental picture measures up to your highest tests, then you are ready to go to God with it. *Do not hesitate.*

2. *Ask.* Read over again the verses I quoted earlier in this chapter about asking. Fix them firmly in your mind, along with the picture which is focused on your mental screen. Then you begin to ask with genuine hope. You never think of saying, "Lord, I want this but I know You would not do it for me." Instead, you take the positive approach. You *know* there is a way for that picture to become reality.

    Many years ago I heard a story that impressed me deeply, and many times I have used this same technique. This story was about a man who, every night when he went to bed, would put his keys in his shoe. The next morning, when he started to put on his shoe, his foot would touch those keys. He would take the keys out and say to himself, "There are doors that are locked, but locked doors will not stop me, because these keys will unlock those doors." Then he would pray, *Lord, when I come up against some situation today— one that seems to be blocking my path—instead of feel-*

ing defeated, let me realize there is a key to every situation, and help me look for and find that key.

3. After you see the picture and after you ask, the third step is *do what you can do.*

    I know a lady who is really an outstanding executive in a corporation. She tells about how she got a job as a stenographer. She wanted to be more than a stenographer, but she realized that she did not have the qualifications. She enrolled in a night school, and began to study accounting and business procedures and other courses that would help her in her work. Working all day, and then going to school at night was not easy. But she kept on, and she learned, and she qualified herself for higher positions. She got those positions.

    The Christian faith is never a shortcut. Often it is an inspiration for you to get up and go to work. God usually takes over after we have done our best.

4. *Let us ask, believing.* We want what is best for our children. The Bible tells us that God wants what is best for us. Let us picture in our minds a Heavenly Father who both knows and loves us. Certainly, that Father does not want anything bad to happen to us. As we concentrate on the goodness of God, we begin to see the possibility of good things coming into our lives. Then it is we surrender our lives to God's will and plan.

I deeply appreciate Lewis Carroll's famous and fantastic masterpiece *Through the Looking Glass.* It contains a story in Chapter 5 that has remained in my mind. There is a conversation between Alice and the Queen, which goes like this:

"I can't believe *that!*" said Alice.

"Can't you?" the Queen said in a pitying tone. "Try again; draw a long breath, and shut your eyes."

Alice laughed. "There's no use trying," she said: "one *can't* believe impossible things."

"I daresay you haven't had much practice," said the Queen. "When I was your age, I always did it for half-an-hour a day. Why, sometimes I've believed as many as six impossible things before breakfast. . . . "

I dearly love the song, but even if I didn't, the title still would be a favorite of mine: "To Dream the Impossible Dream."

One of the elements of believing is doing what you can. I like the spirit of the man who said, "I cannot sing in tune, but at least I can sing with feeling." I have heard some people who could sing, but they did not give the impression that they felt it. If you don't feel it, singing is not very effective.

But just *feeling* is not enough. We must *do* something about it. Believing really includes dreaming, feeling, and action—and really—the order of those is not too important. Some people begin by dreaming, and then begin seeking to make that dream a reality. Others start with doing what they can do, and then develop dreams as they go. The important thing is to begin and go forward. Feelings can bring about dreams. It really does not matter where we begin; what matters is that we *do* begin.

Frequently, I lift up in my mind a phrase of Saint Paul's which inspires me: " . . . for it is the power of God unto salvation to everyone that believeth . . . " (Romans 1:16). I like the association of the words *power* and *believe*. I think they go together. The reason a lot of people lack power is they never learned how to believe.

Edward Everett Hale said it a beautiful way:

> I am only one
> But still I am one.
> I cannot do everything,
> But still I can do something;
> And because I cannot do everything
> I will not refuse to do the
> something that I can do.

First Four Letters of The Alphabet

I find help sometimes in the first four letters of the alphabet:
A, B, C, D.

● *A*—that stands for *ask*. Not only do we ask God for what
we want; we ask God for what *He* wants. There comes a
time in every life—in truth, many times—when we say,
"God what do You want me to do?"
When I feel that my life is in harmony with God's plan,
then I have a sense of security and happiness. I experience
patience and I can even bear pain or unpleasant experiences.
Furthermore, when I feel that I am in God's will, then I am
not jealous of other persons; I am not greedy; I am not
afraid.

● *B*—that stands for *believing*—to believe even "The Impossible Dream." It means to believe *in yourself*—to believe
that there are those who love you and will help you—and
most important—to believe in the goodness and mercy and
power of God.

● *C*—that stands for *commitment*. That means doing something about that which we believe. I heard about a law
professor who was supposed to be an authority on the writing of wills. However, it was discovered after his death that
he, himself, had never made his own will! One wonders how
really committed he was to the importance of making a
will.

● *D*—that means *doing something about it.* We can *ask—*
believe—commit—but until we *do something,* nothing is
really going to happen.

Every Sunday I preach on radio and television. I always
appreciate it when people say to me that they heard me, and
that my message was helpful.

I was especially impressed recently. There is a well-known
store in Houston called Harold's Men's Wear. During this par-

ticular evening, Harold Wiesenthal, who is the owner of that
store, came over to my table and spoke to me. He told me that
he is a Jew, but that every Sunday he listens to me and that
my sermons are helpful. Then he said this, "I want you to come
out to my store. I want to give you a new suit." The point is,
it is much more impressive when we do something about our
convictions.

Ask—believe—commit—and then, *do something*.

10
Try Asking God

For many years, Kate Smith was one of the most inspiring
and charming singers on radio and television. Nobody—and I
mean *nobody*—can sing "God Bless America" as well as she can
sing it. Once she was asked, "Miss Smith, you always seem to
be confident and victorious. What is your philosophy of living?"
She replied that it had been the same since she was a little girl.
Then she told the story of the beginning of her faith:

Once she and two other girls were in a rowboat out on the
Chesapeake Bay. They were having such a good time that they
did not notice that the outgoing tide had swept them far from
the shore, and that it was nearly dark. They rowed as hard as
they could, but could not make progress against the tide. They
were going farther from the shore. They cried for help, but no
one could hear. In the midst of her fear, Kate Smith remembered that the Bible said something about two or three gathering together in His name and asking.

She told her two friends about it, and then she said, "We
have three. God will save us if we ask Him." So they began to

pray, and out of the gathering darkness loomed the lines of a
boat. They were taken on board and carried back to safety.
From that time on, in trouble, in need, in disappointment, in
every circumstance of life, her philosophy has been simply,
"Try asking God."

There are some who might object to this philosophy on the
grounds that it is using your religion for your own good. However, does God object to His children being successful in life? I
have read every word of the New Testament, and I do not recall
one word urging Christians to be failures. We do remember
that Jesus said: "If ye then, being evil, know how to give good
gifts unto your children, how much more shall your Father
which is in heaven give good things to them that ask him?"
(Matthew 7:11). In that same chapter, Jesus also said, "Ask,
and it shall be given you . . . " (7:7). Indeed—why not "try
asking God?"

When We Don't Receive

On the other hand, each one of us can say that we did ask
and did not receive. We remember reading one of the most
delightful books ever written—*The Adventures of Huckleberry
Finn* by Mark Twain.

In that book, Huck said this:

> . . . Miss Watson she took me in the closet and prayed,
> but nothing come of it. She told me to pray every day,
> and whatever I asked for I would get it. But it warn't
> so. I tried it. Once I got a fish-line, but no hooks. It
> warn't any good to me without hooks. I tried for the
> hooks three or four times, but somehow I couldn't make
> it work. By and by, one day, I asked Miss Watson to try
> for me, but she said I was a fool. She never told me why,
> and I couldn't make it out no way.
> I set down one time back in the woods, and had a long
> think about it. I says to myself, if a body can get any-

thing they pray for why don't Deacon Winn get back
the money he lost on pork? Why can't the widow get
back her silver snuff-box that was stole? Why can't
Miss Watson fat up? No, says I to myself, there ain't
nothing in it. . . .

We have prayed for health, and sickness has come; we have
prayed for loved ones to get well, and they have died; we have
prayed for material blessings, but they did not come. Yes, we
have prayed, and we can say with Huckleberry, "Nothing come
of it."

However, in the fourth chapter of the Epistle of James we
read these words: "Ye ask, and receive not, because ye ask
amiss . . . " (v. 3). In that same chapter, James also tells us:
"Submit yourselves therefore to God . . . " (v. 7). And also he
says: "Draw nigh to God, and he will draw nigh to you . . . "
(v. 8). Again, James says: "Humble yourselves in the sight of
the Lord, and he shall lift you up" (v. 10).

A Right Relationship

What we must keep in mind—always—is that asking begins
with a right relationship with God.

I cannot count the times people have said to me, "God does
not seem close to me." Invariably my answer is, "If God is not
close to you, who moved?" The best definition I know of asking
in prayer is the one in the *Westminster Shorter Catechism:*
"Prayer is the offering of our desires unto God for things agree-
able to His will."

That puts the center of our asking God exactly where it
belongs—not on the things *we ask for,* but rather upon *God* and
His will. However, it also allows for the human side of prayer,
that is, *our desires.* When we reach the point in our lives at
which we trust God's ability, His purposes, and His judgments,
then, whatever His answer to our prayer may be, that is the
answer we want; our desires are fulfilled.

Sometimes we are perplexed by life, but there is a poem I learned many, many years ago, which has blessed my heart. It reminds me that—no matter what happens—there are certain basic principles I must abide by. We talk about "losing our faith"; however, there are some things which we believe that —no matter what happens—we keep on believing. So I many times have quoted these words to myself:

> I know that right is right;
> That it is not good to lie;
> That love is better than spite,
> And a neighbor than a spy;
>
> In the darkest night of the year,
> When the stars have all gone out,
> That courage is better than fear,
> That faith is truer than doubt;
>
> And fierce though the fiends may fight;
> And long though the angels hide,
> I know that Truth and Right
> Have the universe on their side;
>
> And that somewhere, beyond the stars,
> Is a Love that is better than fate;
> When the night unlocks her bars
> I shall see Him, and I will wait.
>
> WASHINGTON GLADDEN

God Knows When to Answer

One of the many attributes of God is patience. In the Book of Numbers, there is a verse that we need to read every so often. It goes like this: "The Lord is longsuffering, and of great mercy, forgiving iniquity and transgression . . . " (14:18).

Patience is one of the qualities of God which we need to emphasize. The Bible tells us that God created the world in six days, but the Bible does not tell us exactly how long those days were. Of course, God has the power to create the world in six twenty-four-hour days. On the other hand, those days might have been much, much longer. God could wait a million years or ten million years. The truth of the matter is, God's creation is a constant process.

We think about how long He waited before He sent His Son, Jesus Christ. Paul reminds us that "When the fulness of the time was come, God sent forth his Son . . . " (Galatians 4:4). Now we look again at the patience of God. It has been almost two thousand years since Jesus came. Certainly, one might have expected that His Kingdom would have been established in two thousand years! In two thousand years one might feel that every person on earth would have come to recognize the Son of God, but God is patiently waiting and working. It may take ten thousand years; it may take a hundred thousand years, but God is patient.

I heard a preacher not long ago say that in his church, they did not talk about "backsliding" members because, he explained, in his church most of the members did not get far enough ahead to slide back! But God is patient.

Have Patience

I know some people who let their day be ruined when they miss one section of a revolving door. But sometimes before God answers our askings, we have to wait. A wonderful poet said it beautifully:

> O God, forgive my pettish row!
> I see Your job . . .
> ....
> Man won't come right!
> After Your patient centuries,
> Fresh starts, recasting, tired Gethsemanes
> And tense Golgothas, he, Your central theme,

Is just a jangling echo of Your dream . . .
Why don't You quit?
Crumple it all and dream again!
But no;
Flaw after flaw, You work it out, revise, refine—
Bondage, brutality, and war, and woe,
The sot, the fool, the tyrant and the mob—
Dear God, how You must love Your job!

BADGER CLARK
"The Job"

Also, there is a sentence in the Book of James which I have read many times. Let me quote it from the New English Bible: " . . . The farmer looking for the precious crop his land may yield can only wait in patience, until the autumn and spring rains have fallen" (James 5:7). One of the best examples of patience in our society is the farmer.

But we do not like to be patient. We have our own timetables; we want things done on *our* schedules. We forget that in his *Othello,* Shakespeare said, "What wound did ever heal but by degrees?" We want our wounds to heal instantly—not only the wounds of our bodies, but the wounds of our hearts and our spirits.

There is a Jewish proverb which says it graphically: "If you would plant for yourself, plant the grapevine; if you plant for your children, plant the fig tree; but if you plant for your children's children, plant the olive tree." Sometimes we need to think and plan generations ahead.

It has been well said: "Wait and see." Sometimes we cannot see *except* by waiting. As we "have patience with the patience of God," we find our own patience strengthened.

11

Quotients

When I studied psychology in college we heard a lot about *IQ—intelligence quotient.* We learned that some people seemed to have more intelligence—mental ability—than others. During my college days, I put great store on *IQ.*

However, as years have gone by and as I have seen more of life and understood more about people, I have learned that there are some other "quotients" that are important. For example:

- *DQ—drive quotient.* This may be just as important or even more important than *IQ.* On an office wall the other day I saw these words: MY GET UP AND GO HAS GOT UP AND GONE. Some people never really exercise their "get up and go," and a lot of times we lose it. Sometimes we lose our drive in life because of disappointment, or illness, or sorrow, or defeat. And sometimes we lose our drive because we have accomplished all of our dreams. We have no more hills to climb.
- *CQ—creativity quotient* is another very important part of life—the ability to imagine, to think up new ways of doing things, to see other roads when the road we are traveling has been blocked.

- *AQ—awareness quotient* is another great human need. We need to be aware of our own selves—the reason why we feel hurt, or thwarted, or defeated. We need to be aware of our own needs, and how those needs can be met. *Awareness* also applies to other people. A man and wife can live together day after day and month after month—and never really be aware of each other. A parent may never really become aware of a child.
- *PQ—patience quotient* is also very important. We have been discussing that in these preceding pages, but it needs to be constantly emphasized. Our patience level can be very low.
- *LQ—love quotient* is really important. The ability to love is probably the greatest ability that mankind possesses. I have a poem which was written in 1908. Early in my life I discovered this poem, and through the years I have read it many times. I think it says it as beautifully and completely as any that I know. Read with me again these words:

TEACH ME TO LOVE

There was a time when in my daily prayer
I asked for all the things I deemed most fair,
And necessary to my life,—success,
Riches, of course, and ease, and happiness;
A host of friends, a home without alloy;
A primrose path of luxury and joy,
Social distinction, and enough of fame
To leave behind a well-remembered name.

Ambition ruled my life. I longed to do
Great things, that all my little world might view
And whisper, "Wonderful!"

Ah, patient God,
How blind we are, until Thy shepherd's rod
Of tender chastening gently leads us on

To better things! Today I have but one
Petition, Lord—Teach me to love. Indeed,
It is my greatest and my only need—
Teach me to love, not those who first love me,
But all the world, with that rare purity
Of broad, outreaching thought which bears no trace
Of earthly taint, but holds in its embrace
Humanity, and only seems to see
The good in all, reflected, Lord, from Thee.
And teach me, Father, how to love the most
Those who most stand in need of love—that host
Of people who are sick and poor and bad,
Whose tired faces show their lives are sad,
Who toil along the road with footsteps slow,
And hearts more heavy than the world can know—
People whom others pass discreetly by,
Or fail to hear the pleading of that cry
For help, amid the tumult of the crowd;
Whose very anguish makes them cold and proud,
Resentful, stubborn, bitter in their grief—
I want to bring them comfort and relief,
To put my hand in theirs, and at their side
Walk softly on, a faithful, fearless guide.
O Saviour, thou the Christ, Truth, ever near,
Help me to feel these sad ones doubly dear
Because they need so much! Help me to seek
And find that which they thought was lost; to speak
Such words of cheer that as we pass along
The wilderness shall blossom into song.

Ah, Love divine, how empty was that prayer
Of other days! That which was once so fair,—
Those flimsy baubles which the world calls joys
Are nothing to me now but broken toys,
Outlived, outgrown. I thank Thee that I know
Those much-desired dreams of long ago,

Like butterflies, have had their summer's day
Of brief enchantment, and have gone. I pray
For better things.
>   Thou knowest, God above,
My one desire now—Teach me to love.
>   LOUISE WHEATLEY COOK HOVNANIAN

12

Past, Present, Future

Just at this point, I feel inspired to put down for our consideration some words that Saint Paul said, which I feel have never been said better: " . . . forgetting those things which are behind, and reaching forth unto those things which are before, I press toward the mark . . . " (Philippians 3:13, 14). One of the great difficulties in loving ourselves is our remembering the past—mistakes, sins, failures, et cetera, et cetera, and on and on.

A minister friend of mine tells the story of one day seeing a fruit tree blown over in a farmer's field, through which he was walking. It happened that the farmer was nearby. He asked him what happened to the tree, and the farmer explained that a heavy wind had blown it over and uprooted it. My friend said, "What are you going to do with it?" The farmer made a wonderful reply. He declared, "You see it has fruit on the branches. I am going to gather the fruit, and then burn the tree."

That is a tremendous philosophy of life. There are many experiences, relationships, situations in our lives that have been uprooted. Every one of those experiences has some fruit, which we can gather.

Through the years I have counseled with numerous people in reference to the death of a loved one. Over and over we have talked about how we can reap the benefits of that person's life —how we can remember all of the good, inspiring, and happy results of that person's having lived.

The same can be said of so many other experiences which have been now "uprooted." Every tragedy in the past still has some fruit on it. Let us use the philosophy of the farmer: "Gather the fruit, and then burn the tree." That is, take what is good from the past, but do not be bound to that which is going to do nothing but rot and decay.

We have made mistakes. "Let us gather the fruit and burn the tree." Life has a way of cutting and hurting and sometimes scars are left. However, let us remember that they *are* scars and not fresh wounds.

It is not God's design that we hold on to yesterday's sin. It is both beautiful and comforting to read the words of the Psalmist, "As far as the east is from the west, so far hath he removed our transgressions from us" (Psalms 103:12). God does not intend for us to live forever with a rotting tree. Even though it was a sin, there is some fruit which we can gather from it.

The Road Not Taken

Not only past sins, but also past regrets must be dealt with. Over and over we say, "If I had only done this," or, "If I had only done that." Let us always remind ourselves that we do not know what was on that other road.

Many of us remember these wonderful lines of Robert Frost:

> Two roads diverged in a yellow wood,
> And sorry I could not travel both
> And be one traveller, long I stood
> And looked down one as far as I could

To where it bent in the undergrowth;
Then took the other. . . .

However, even as we look back upon decisions we wish we had made, we gather the fruit. We have learned from our experiences; other opportunities will come—and then, we burn the tree. The past was meant to be a guidepost, not a hitching post! When driving your car, if you keep your eyes glued on the rearview mirror, you will see where you have been—but you likely will end up a wreck in some ditch. It is good to glance at the rearview mirror from time to time, but it is also good to keep your eyes on the road ahead.

The important thing to remember—and thank God for—is that in spite of what we did yesterday, there are still steps that can be taken today, and there is still a tomorrow.

Time and again, we need to be reminded to "burn the tree." The past can bring so much bitterness. We can give our lives in retaliation, rather than in reconciliation.

All of us who have ever been to the theater are familiar with the names Gilbert and Sullivan. How their words and music have inspired multitudes of people! But there is a very sad story about them. For years, Gilbert would send Sullivan the words by mail, and Sullivan would send Gilbert the music by mail. When they had an opening night, they would stand at opposite ends of the stage and bow facing forward, so that they would not ever need to look at each other. The problem was that they had a falling out over the purchase of a new carpet in one of their theaters, and they never settled that grudge. Two men with creative imaginations—who brought so much happiness to the world—so nourished a grudge. What a tragedy!

There is an Arab proverb which goes like this: WRITE THE WRONGS THAT ARE DONE TO YOU IN SAND; BUT WRITE THE GOOD THINGS THAT HAPPEN TO YOU ON A PIECE OF MARBLE. Let go all of such emotions as resentment and retaliation, which diminish you, and hold on to the emotions, such as gratitude and joy, which increase you.

To me, one of the saddest scenes in all the Bible is not that Simon Peter denied Jesus, but rather, that he had to watch Him being crucified, believing he would never have the opportunity to talk with Jesus again. We have that same experience. We have loved ones that are now in some grave, and how we wish we could talk with them about something that one of us did or said!

And then we remember that after Jesus rose from the dead, sitting at breakfast with Simon Peter, Jesus simply said, "Peter, do you love me?" (*See* John 21:15.) In that moment, they both knew it was not necessary to say anything more about the past. They both realized it was time to start over and go on. And so, Jesus said to Simon Peter, " . . . Feed my sheep" (v. 16). That is, look to the future and keep living. When we think of those loved ones and recall those experiences we would like to live over, really, even if we had the opportunity, we know there is no need to go back; we need to go forward: *Gather the fruit and burn the tree.*

Today Is Tomorrow's Yesterday

Speaking of the past, we need to remind ourselves that today is going to be tomorrow's past. There is tremendous power in freeing ourselves from the distractions of both yesterday and tomorrow, and convincing ourselves that we have this day at our disposal. What can I do *this* day to make it the best day— one I can look back on tomorrow?

Paul said, "The last enemy that shall be destroyed is death" (1 Corinthians 15:26). If you study that chapter, you can determine pretty well what he means when he says that; but in another respect, I never have thought of death as an enemy. I do know that some day I am not going to have a tomorrow.

I am thinking at this moment of my older brother, Stanley F. Allen, who lived in Goodman, Mississippi. He was in the hospital with a terminal illness. However, he never realized it was terminal, and was constantly thinking about the future.

One night he phoned me and talked for a good while about our taking a trip together to England. He had been reading a book about England that night. Later on that very night he died. I think it was glorious that he died looking toward tomorrow.

On the other hand, we also need to face the fact that there may not be a tomorrow on this earth. We know there is a tomorrow beyond this earth, but each day we need to say with the Psalmist, "This is the day which the Lord hath made; we will rejoice and be glad in it" (Psalms 118:24). The only day I have is today. Let me make something good and joyful out of this one day. It is a tragic waste to dissipate this moment's energy by thinking about yesterday or tomorrow. There is a time to remember, there is a time to dream—but there is also a time to live in the here and now. There is great power in trusting ourselves to the moment in which we are now living.

I now give my vacation times to leading small groups to the Holy Land. I have been to the Holy Land many times. Each time is a new and fresh and wonderful experience. It is interesting to watch the people who carry their cameras. I am not opposed to taking pictures, and I think pictures are beautiful and wonderful, but I have come to believe that taking pictures to be looked at tomorrow can become so important that we miss seeing the view today.

How can one describe the moment of kneeling at the rock where Jesus knelt in Gethsemane; or sitting upon the deck of a ship that is sailing across the Sea of Galilee; or looking out across the fields where the shepherds were keeping watch over their flocks by night, and the angel of the Lord came upon them; or standing at the well in Nazareth where Mary, the mother of Jesus, came to get water—and on and on. I am happy for people to take pictures, but also I urge the people with me to not be distracted from the experience of that moment. I sometimes think that those of us who sit or stand in silence, often catch the beauty and inspiration far more than those who use their energies in trying to preserve that moment.

In the church where I am the minister, we have an average

of three weddings every week. Photographers come and take pictures, and I know those pictures are important. Many times those pictures will be handed down to children and to grandchildren, but I also know that the experience that couple has as they stand at the altar is a glorious moment.

Perhaps we ought not to try to preserve the present. Maybe we ought to just experience the moment and not think about tomorrow. Anne Morrow Lindbergh once said in *Gift From the Sea:* "We have so little faith in the ebb and flow of life, of love, of relationships . . . We insist on permanancy, on duration, on continuity; when the only continuity possible, in life as in love, is in growth, in fluidity—in freedom. . . . "

There is a Latin phrase *carpe diem*. It means "seize the moment."

Some people are so busy worrying about yesterday or tomorrow, that they miss today. We need to tune in on the voices and impulses which are all around us at this very moment.

Dr. William E. Sangster was a great minister in Britain, until his death a few years ago. He tells this incident: One morning he was working in his study in his church in London. Suddenly he felt an impulse to make a pastoral call on a woman who was a member of his church. He had other appointments that day, and he really did not know why he should call on this particular woman, but he obeyed the impulse of the moment.

When he knocked at the door she greeted him with a beautiful smile and said, "It is wonderful that you remembered."

Dr. Sangster replied that he did not know anything that he should have remembered. However, she continued speaking, "It was exactly one year ago today that you conducted the funeral of my dear husband. I have been dreading this day, and I felt like getting out and running away. I kept feeling that I should stay here, however, and wait within the house. If I had left, I would have missed your visit."

Dr. Sangster honestly confessed to the woman that he had not remembered, but that he had felt an impulse to come to see her not knowing why he so felt. Then she made a wonderful observation: "Truly, God must keep a calendar!"

The point is, it is marvelous to be so alive at the moment that we can feel the impulses all about us. If we ever expect to live, we must live in the "now."

We Are Not Alone

Another thought: *We are not alone at this moment.*

When Dietrich Ritschl, the German theologian, was in this country after the war, he recalled a desperate night in 1944 when he was caught in a bombing attack that claimed more than a thousand lives. He said:

> After the worst was over, I found myself lying in the waiting room of a railroad station. The roof was cracked; I saw the flames going up, and my eyes caught an inscription up there—a quotation from the poet Schiller: HIGH BEYOND ALL STARS SURELY DWELLS A LOVING FATHER.
>
> Then I said to myself, "To hell with this father; I don't want to have him." And I hope you say the same. I hope you are not worshipping someone who hovers above the clouds and does not care for us. I hope you have heard of him who is with us where the bombs fall, where the Iron Curtains are, where all courage, confidence and strength are gone. I hope you know that there he is, and he is nowhere else. He mixes with us. He is one of us. *He goes with us into baptism of repentance.* Even before he speaks, even before he says anything, even before he demands anything of us, he comes and is with us.
>
> He comes in human terms and mixes with people. He repents with them in solidarity. He is not above them; he is with them. And this ministry, which began with his baptism, will lead him to even lower levels. Finally his humiliation and shame were complete . . . it is dark

and muddy, where it stinks, and where you and I could
not stand to live—if it were not for him. This is his way,
because he wanted to take it all upon his shoulders.

536,870,912 PENNIES

This idea of "living today" may seem very narrow. However,
never underestimate the cumulative effect of days that we live.
Take for example one penny. If you see a penny lying on the
sidewalk, you hardly feel it is worth the effort to bend over and
pick it up. But suppose you began to double that penny each day
for a month. At the end of a week, you would only have sixty-
four pennies. That's not very impressive—but at the end of a
month you would have 536,870,912 pennies. Translated into
dollars that would be $5,368,709.12—more than five million
dollars.

One moment may not seem important in one day, but as we
begin to multiply those moments, it is astounding how many we
would have in one month. My little calculator could not even
approach telling me how many moments we would have in a
year, and it is utterly beyond a person's imagination to think
about how many moments could be added up in a lifetime.

Someone tells of watching a stonecutter bang away at the
stone with his hammer and wedge. He might hit the stone a
hundred times with no apparent effect, but on the hundred and
first lick, the stone would crack. The point is, the hundred and
first blow did not crack the stone by itself; it was the cumulative
effect of the hundred blows *before* which brought the results.

That is the way our moments and our days work. Sometimes
it seems we make no progress; sometimes it seems all of our
efforts are useless, but we keep trying; we struggle without
giving up. Then one day, the victory we have sought belongs to
us. It was not that final effort—it was all those efforts that went
before.

That is why we pray to God in the words of the beautiful

hymn written by Harry Emerson Fosdick:

> Grant us wisdom, grant us courage,
> For the living of these days. . . .

Someone has wisely said, "Today is the tomorrow that we worried about yesterday, and yet, all is well." We have heard it said again and again that "tomorrow never comes." We really do not believe it. The trouble is, many of us not only believe that tomorrow *will* come, we also are afraid it will come without us. But as we look back, we see that—up to now—we have been here when each new day of our lives dawns.

The writings of Thoreau have meant so much to me. When he was spending some time alone at Walden Pond, he said this: "Little man, why do you get so hot and bothered—because all the stars are still in their place." As we look back, it is amazing how God brought us from the past, and still sustains us in the present. That being true, we can believe in God's unbelievable capacity to uphold us, as we face the future.

I have spent many hours flying on airplanes. It used to be that I wanted to sit next to a window, so I could watch the sky ahead. If I saw what might be turbulent weather coming up, I would become very nervous. But through the years I have been through some rather heavy turbulence, and I have come to realize that *we got through.* Little by little, I have decided that there is nothing I can do about the weather ahead, that we have a capable pilot, and I determined to quit worrying about turbulence! That has been a great blessing to me in my air travels. Today, if I sit next to the window, it is to see the scenery and not to worry about the turbulence.

Maybe this is a good philosophy in life. So many times we miss the scenery today, worrying about the turbulence ahead.

The Stone

One of the Bible stories that I often quote is the story of the three women who were going to the tomb of Jesus very early on Sunday morning. It was in the springtime of the year, and I am sure that beautiful wild flowers were growing along the way. But they missed the beauty of those flowers. Perhaps the sun was just rising, but they missed seeing that great light, as it gradually drove the darkness from all around them. They missed the glory and beauty of the beginning of a new day, because they were asking one question, "Who shall roll away the stone from the door of the sepulcher?" They were worrying about a problem ahead. Perhaps they were feeling that removing the huge stone was an impossible task—that it would forever block the door to the tomb of Christ. However, when they arrived at the tomb, they found the stone had already been rolled away, and later they discovered that their Master was now alive.

Couples, as they grow older, have a way of saying, "Who will roll away the stone, when my wife [or husband] dies?" Yet, to most couples, that experience comes to one or the other, and the other one does go on living. A student has a way of saying, "Who will roll away the stone, when I fail the examination?" Somehow, stones get rolled away, and students become men and women and take their place in society. You can name any problem in your life and ask the question, "Who will roll away the stone?"

One could translate Jesus' words to read, "Do not fret about tomorrow because, with tomorrow's energy, you will always be able to solve tomorrow's problems" (*see* Matthew 6:34). That is a very revealing and wonderful sentence. We think about the problems of tomorrow, but we forget about the new energies which we will have, when those problems come. You do not have the strength or the ability today that you will have tomorrow. Tomorrow you will have what you need.

I love the words of Fay Foster's song "My Journey's End."

Ain't this a terrible world, O Lord!
Ain't this a terrible world, O Lord!
Where's there quiet, where's there peace, O Lord?
There's moaning and sighing and hating and lying,
There's shouting and crying and shooting and dying—
Where's there pity, where's there love, O Lord?

You say there's a place called journey's end,
A place called Heaven, too,
Where we are all each other's friend,
And there ain't no work to do?

Why, thank you, Lord, thank you! That's very encouraging.
O Lord, show me that place
That you're telling me of,
Where there ain't no creed or race,
And all is brotherly love.

What's that you say, Lord?
I've got to spread the brotherly love down here,
    to poor sinners, before I gets the call?
Yes, Lord!

Maybe this world ain't bad, at all, I'll patiently wait
    till I gets the call,
I'll find quiet; I'll find peace, O Lord.
With praying and preaching the Gospel, and teaching
Each brother and sister to love one another.

There'll be light! There'll be glory, dear Lord! . . .
And when for the last time I lay me down to sleep,
Dear Lord, please send the angels to get me and take
    me and lead me,
To my journey's end. I'll wake up at my journey's end!

13

Failures Are Never Final

Recently, I clipped from the newspaper a story, which I would like to quote at some length. I think it is wonderful, and it applies in some degree and in some way to every one of us. The title in the newspaper was, ARCHITECT, INVENTOR BUCKMINSTER FULLER ONCE FAILURE, DRUNK. Then the story follows:

Architect and inventor Buckminster Fuller, beset by a family tragedy, was a failure and a drunk in 1927, when he decided to throw himself into Lake Michigan and commit suicide.

Five years earlier, his first daughter had died on her fourth birthday after suffering infantile paralysis, flu, spinal meningitis, and pneumonia.

After his daughter's death, his company failed, Fuller said in an interview in the latest issue of *Quest-79* magazine, "I'd go off and drink all night."

Fuller and his wife were living in a one-room apartment in Chicago, and he was well acquainted with Lincoln Park, right on Lake Michigan.

"So I knew just where to go when I decided to throw myself into the lake, fully intending to commit suicide," he said.

Standing there, Fuller told himself: "You do not have the right to eliminate yourself. You do not belong to you. You belong to the universe."

Fuller, who later would invent the geodesic dome and become known as an architect, engineer, futurist, cartographer and author, said he vowed to live on "to do my own thinking" and "to apply my inventory of experience to the solving of problems that affect everyone aboard planet Earth."

"I didn't waste a second," he said, "I slept the way certain animals sleep: lying down as soon as I was tired, sleeping a half-hour every six hours.

"I also decided to hold a moratorium on speech. It was very tough on my wife, but for two years in that Chicago tenement I didn't allow myself to use words. I wanted to force myself back to the point where I could understand what I was thinking."

Fuller, now 84, said he decided to forget about earning a living, instead committing himself to "the invention and development of physical artifacts to reform the environment."

"It became obvious to me that if I worked always and only for all humanity, I would be optimally effective. I'd be doing what nature wanted me to do, and nature literally would support me," he said.

In 1928, Fuller invented the "4-D" house, a self-contained dustless unit, transportable by air. There followed the streamlined Dymaxion auto in 1933 and the Dymaxion house in 1944-45, utilizing Fuller's principle of maximum output from a minimum of material and energy.

The principle is illustrated in his geodesic domes, spherical structures constructed of lightweight but extremely strong triangular parts.

"Many times I've chickened," Fuller said, "and everything inevitably goes wrong. But then, when I return to my commitment, my life suddenly works again. There's something of the miraculous in all that."

JOHN LOVE

Win or Lose

More and more we are living in a "win or lose" culture. Years ago, the great sportswriter, Grantland Rice said that it was not important whether you win or lose, but "how you played the game." However, our society today does not accept that. The important point *is* whether we win or lose. The hope for success and the fear of failure are probably the two greatest burdens that mankind bears today. In a society of superstars and celebrities in every field, we feel the pressure to be on the winning side somewhere—in our homes—in school—at the office—in our social contacts—or in some contact in life.

The truth of the matter, however, is that we do lose, and many times we complain and feel deeply hurt. I like the philosophy that someone expressed:

> Don't complain about the way the ball bounces, if you
> are the one who dropped the ball.

One of my favorite pastimes is watching football on television, and one of my favorite announcers is Don Meredith. I have liked him ever since he played football in college, and I think he is really a fine person. During a football game the announcer said, "If the quarterback had just thrown to the man on the other side of the field, they would have scored a touchdown."

Don Meredith spoke up and made an observation that I have kept in my mind and really found comfort in. He said:

> If *ifs* and *buts* were candy and nuts, we'd all have a
> Merry Christmas.

But you can't live your life with *ifs* and *buts*.

We can spend our lives asking the wrong questions. Instead of asking, "Why did I drop the ball?" it is easier to ask, "Why was my friend disloyal?" "Why was my mate unfaithful?" "Why was my professor unreasonable?" "Why didn't my boss understand me?" "Why did I get caught in this situation?" And on and on. The questions can be directed—always—to some-body else. We need to remind ourselves that instead of com-plaining about how the ball bounces, we should face up to the fact that "I dropped the ball."

The truth of the matter is, failure can be a wonderful experi-ence. It means that you were willing to take a chance, even with the possibilities of failure. The greatest tragedy in life is that of the person who is never willing to risk anything. You do not win in life because you never make mistakes. The truth of the matter is, the more mistakes you make, the more victori-ous you will be. Because by taking risks, you gain victories. Psychologists have told us for years that the "fear of failure" is the reason that so many of us never try. When you get up the nerve to really face up to that beast we call *failure* and not be frightened by it, then you are on the road to accomplishment.

No person likes to fail, but to fail is better than not to try at all.

We also need to learn that no matter how heartbreaking the failure, life goes on. We *celebrate* victories, but we *reflect* on failures.

When I lived in Atlanta, Georgia, it was a happy privilege to belong to the East Lake Country Club. I spent many happy hours there. The great golfer Bobby Jones was a member of that club, and I saw him frequently. One day I heard him make this observation: "I never learned anything from a golf tourna-ment that I won. I learned golf from the tournaments I lost." We never learn from celebrating victory.

"He Simply Got Up and Left"

Arnold Bennett's *Journal* is not something that I recom-mend reading. The truth is, it is very dull. However, Arnold Bennett made one entry that I find very stirring and inspiring. Under the date of March 9, 1928, he writes: "John Buchan, invited for tea at four-thirty, arrived at four-twenty-seven. He

is a thoroughly organized man. And at five-fifteen, he simply
got up and left."

That phrase *he simply got up and left* is wonderful. One of
the things we need to learn is how to leave. Remember this—
if you ever expect to go anywhere, you must leave somewhere.
You cannot both stay and go.

Let Your Anchor Down

For many years I have been the minister of a large church
in the center of a city. I have found there are many unhappy
people in a city, simply because they do not want to live there;
they want to be back yonder where they used to live.

I grew up in Georgia, and I learned to love that state very
much. Then, one August, we moved from Georgia to Texas. I
never shall forget a lady saying to me, "Are you all going home
for Christmas?" My reply was, "Lady, we *are* at home." As
much as I love Georgia, when we moved, we moved. You cannot
live in two places at the same time.

The tragedy of many, many people in every city is right at
this point. They did not know how to leave the last place they
lived.

I once heard of an old ship captain who said, "Even if I am
in port for only one day, I let my anchor down." And I say to
people that even if you are going to live for a short time, wherever you are, live there that time. We can think so much of
where we were that we forget where we are!

When we are thinking of the past, our minds play tricks on
us. For example, we can have a picnic and during the picnic it
rains; ants and other insects get on the food; mosquitoes bite us,
and really, there is more misery than joy. But years later, as
we look back, we forget about the rain the bugs, and the mosquitoes, and we remember what a happy picnic we had. The
same thing is true about life. I talked to a couple recently who
do not like the city where they are now living. They told me
about the city where they did live, and how wonderful it was.

I have visited that city quite a few times, and know a little about it. We kept talking about it, and the longer we talked, the more convinced they became that the first city is really better than the present one. The problem is in their memories; they are forgetting the unhappy associations about the city they were forced to leave. It is very tempting to glorify yesterday.

"Then Laugh"

Along this same line, we also remember the unhappy times: when we have been wronged; when we have done wrong; when we have been hurt; disappointments; sorrows, and on and on. Memories are never completely wiped out, but they can be controlled. Then we are not controlled by the memories of our past. This is what forgiveness is. This is what God's grace is. Remembering does not have to always be remorse. Memories of past failure may humble us but no longer humiliate us. I like a poem that I clipped somewhere recently. It goes like this:

THEN LAUGH

Build for yourself a strong box,
  Fashion each part with care;
When it's strong as your hand can make it,
  Put all your troubles there;
Hide there all thought of your failures,
  And each bitter cup that you quaff;
Lock all your heartaches within it,
  Then sit on the lid and laugh.

Tell no one else its contents,
  Never its secrets share;
When you've dropped in your care and worry—
  Keep them forever there;

Hide them from sight so completely
  That the world will never dream half;

Fasten the strong box securely—
Then sit on the lid and laugh.

BERTHA ADAMS BACKUS

Don't Turn Back

Sometimes we need to ask ourselves this question, "If I could be born again as a baby and start my life over, would I do it?" I have a feeling that most of us would want to be just left alone, even where we are. We enjoy and have happy memories of our childhood. Going to elementary school was fun; we might even remember with happiness our fourth-grade teacher. Many of us get out our high-school annuals, look again at the pictures of our classmates, and remember delightful experiences; but most of us have no desire to go back and start in the first grade and go through it all again.

We who are older remember with such great joy when our babies were born and their growing up. Sometimes we turn through the family picture album with happy memories. For our children to be babies again, however, is not what we want. We are glad that they are grown, that they have their own homes, and their own families, and are making their own lives.

It has been well said: "Blessed are the young people for they shall inherit the national debt." At first, we feel sorry for them, but, then we have a feeling that they will be able to handle it. God bless them! We had our chance of being young people, and we do not want to go through it again.

It has also been well put: "We talk about the 'good old days' but in truth, they never were."

While we cannot go back and start over again, physically, it is possible for a person to make a fresh beginning. We need to believe that. There are relationships that can be changed; there are habits that can be left behind; there are deeds that can be done, which were left undone.

14
Pain Is Pain

One of the facts about a human being is the ability to feel pain, to be hurt. The truth of the matter is, we are thankful for this ability. Suppose you were to stick a pin in your finger, and you felt no pain. Immediately you would know that something was wrong. Likewise, if sorrow or disappointment or defeats, or whatever, did not cause us to feel pain and hurt, we would know there was something wrong. Be thankful that you *can* be hurt.

In his book *The Problem of Pain*, C. S. Lewis says that pain tells us that something is wrong and needs diagnosis and healing. He further explains, "God whispers to us in our pleasure, speaks in our conscience, but shouts in our pains."

The trouble is, many people fail to get the message, and instead of a *message*, pain itself becomes a disease. Instead of letting pain be a signal to change, or to seek a remedy, it can become possessive of us, and we only feel the pain and nothing beyond it.

Most of the pain comes out of a distortion of good. There are certain good portions in our lives—pleasure, food and drink, money and position, comfort and power, and many others. If we are not careful, these "things" can take control over us, and we make them our goals and our gods. The first step in eliminating needless pain in our lives is to realize that we are not dependent on outside circumstances.

You Cannot Explain It

There are some pains that come through what we call natural disasters. For example, in 1976, an estimated 655,000 people were killed in the great Chinese earthquake. How can you explain such a catastrophe? The answer is that *you cannot explain it*. There are occurrences that we just have to accept without understanding.

A parent learns that a child has been killed in an automobile accident. The pain in that parent's heart is utterly indescribable. Here, also, the question *why* is unanswerable. In circumstances of life, over and over, we feel the pain without knowing the answer.

On the other hand, there is some pain that we actually choose. Listen to these words:

> In stripes above measure, in prisons more frequent, in deaths oft. Five times I have received at the hands of the Jews the forty lashes less one. Three times I have been shipwrecked; a night and a day I have been adrift at sea; on frequent danger from robbers, danger from my own people, danger from Gentiles, danger in the city, danger in the wilderness, danger at sea, danger from false brethren; in toil and hardship, hunger and thirst, often without food, in cold and exposure.
>
> *See* 2 Corinthians 11: 23-27

Those were the words of the most faithful Christian minister that ever lived on this earth. He did not have to suffer as he did; he could have stayed at home in ease and comfort, but he felt a call, a duty, a responsibility, and a purpose in his life.

If we did not love other people, if we did not feel a sense of duty and a call to service, then much of the pain and hurt of life would be taken away. The joys and triumphs of life would be taken away, too. If there is to be joy, there must also be pain. If there is to be victory, there must also be defeat. Read again these words, "Greater love hath no man than this, that a man lay down his life for his friends" (John 15:13). Love causes people to sacrifice and to suffer. We would not have it any other way. One night I was having dinner with Mr. and Mrs. Bernard Sakowitz of Houston. During the dinner she said something that I shall never forget:

> Say everything is well with you—
> And God will listen and make it true.

Somehow, I believe that. At times it is hard to believe it, but eventually, we will see it.

It Is Not the Circumstance: It Is You

Time and again, we blame the problems of life upon circumstance, when all the time, it is not the circumstance—it is ourselves. We cannot control circumstances, but we *can* accept responsibility for ourselves.

Earlier I mentioned that Jesus realized that His life was drawing near the close. He was very anxious about the attitude of those who were closest to Him. He asked them, " . . . Whom do men say that I the Son of man am?" (Matthew 16:13).

That is an easy question to answer. It is not difficult to talk about what other people think; to comment on what other people do; to spend our lives looking at other people and making judgments. We can talk about what the government does; and about public morality; we can talk about the great social issues and what ought to be done about them; we can talk about the economic problems. The truth is, it's easy to talk and think about what's going on in the world. We can get upset about what *other* people are doing.

Then, Jesus asked His friends a second question: "But whom say ye that I am?" (v. 15).

That is the difficult question! That is, what do I think—or believe—or do—or am?

One of the serious mistakes parents make is they are never

willing to let their children assume responsibility for themselves. We have all known parents who sought to direct every thought, word, and deed for their children. I have been in homes and asked some child a question, but the mother would quickly say, "Tell him————." If I had wanted to know what the mother thought, I would have asked her. Let the child answer the question. Let the child make the decision. There are some parents that never know when to quit directing. Even when children get married, there are parents who try to direct their homes and how they rear their children. Many marriages have actually broken up because of interfering parents.

Responsibility for Ourselves

God is much wiser than we are. He is willing for us to answer some questions ourselves. He is willing for us to assume some responsibility for ourselves.

Each of us recognizes the necessity of some self-responsibility. It is not easy to achieve, however. I mentioned Bobby Jones, the great golfer. He started playing golf when he was five years old, and by the time he was twelve years old, he was really an accomplished golfer. However, it was said of him that he would never win the big tournaments because he would always beat himself. He was noted for his temper. If he missed a shot, he would become very upset, and he was known as a club thrower. He entered the national amateur tournament at the age of fourteen, and at that time, he was a good enough golfer to win the tournament. Actually, it was seven years before he finally won it. Someone said of him, "He was fourteen years old when he mastered the game of golf; he was twenty-one years old before he mastered himself."

We can blame our parents, the circumstances of our lives, and many, many other things for our own weaknesses, failures, and insecurities. Eventually, we need to face the fact that *we* are our own worst enemies, and we need to turn those enemies into friends. We need to become our own friends—to learn to love ourselves—to believe that we are *somebodies*.

As we begin to believe in ourselves, we begin to see opportunities in life. But every opportunity involves a risk. If a little baby wants to learn to walk, he has to take the risk of falling. The parent must be willing for the baby to take that risk. On through life, in school, in work, in love, and on and on, there is the principle that we must take responsibility for ourselves. We make decisions and go on. There are times when those decisions do not turn out right, but still we go on. You can't spend your life regretting what happened yesterday.

Rudyard Kipling says it best in his wonderful poem "If":

> If you can make one heap of all your winnings
> And risk it on one turn of pitch-and-toss,
> And lose, and start again at your beginnings
> And never breathe a word about your loss. . . .

The last line of the poem is:

> And—which is more—you will be a Man, my son!

It is difficult to lose and start again without talking about our losses, but that is what it takes to really grow up as persons.

To me, Charles A. Lindbergh has always been a hero. I think the reason I have looked up to him is because he was willing to say, "I will get in that plane alone and take off and fly off across the Atlantic." There was nobody else with him to help him, if he got into trouble. He took the responsibility, and that is the kind of people that fly across the ocean of life.

Our Real Resources

A man was telling me the other day that he had spent some time putting down all of his material assets and adding them up to see what he was worth. For most of us, that would not be an arduous task, because most of us do not have a great amount of material resources. The thought, however, leads me to another kind of checking on ourselves. What are our *real* resources? We can see, we can hear, we can think, we can walk, we live in a world of opportunities. Let us ask ourselves the question, "What powers do I really possess?"

So the real moment comes when we decide what powers we possess, and we decide that we will be responsible people.

15

The Cure for an Inferiority Complex

Years ago when I was in college, majoring in psychology, the three psychologists that I admired the most were Freud, Jung, and Adler. In answer to the question, "What is the one thing people want more than anything else?" each of these great psychologists had a different answer.

Freud's answer was—"To be loved."

Jung's answer was—"To be secure."

Adler's answer was—"To feel important."

Through many years of dealing with people, I have come to agree with Adler. I feel that more than anything else, a person wants to count for something—to feel that he or she amounts to something.

However, the one great obstacle to feeling important is our feeling of unimportance. To some degree, every person feels inferior, and in seeking to overcome that feeling of inferiority, we do a lot of things—some wrong and some right.

Six Wrong Methods

First, let me mention *six wrong methods* we use to overcome an inferiority complex.

1. *We can use the "smoke-screen" method.* That is, feeling inferior we become abnormally aggressive, boastful, dictatorial, and the like. There is a tendency to put on a show—always calling attention to ourselves.

2. *There is the "sour-grape" method.* We remember Aesop's fable of the fox who jumped and jumped, trying to reach the grapes. Finally, he gave up, saying, "The grapes are sour anyway." A frail youth may discount athletics. Certain people may seek to put down intellectuals, calling them "highbrows." It is easy to feign a lack of interest in the things we cannot reach, and say they are not worthwhile.

3. *"Daydreaming" is another route.* It is possible to live in a world of fantasy. Unable to face the real world, we can retreat into a dream world. The tragedy of many people is that they satisfy their ambitions in their dreams.
    Something that has had a profound influence upon my life was a statement that a teacher in a high-school English class made one day. I never have forgotten it. The statement was: "I would rather be a good ditchdigger, than dream of building Panama Canals and never do anything."

4. *"Excuses" constitute another formula.* We remember the story that Jesus told of the man who gave his servants the talents to care for and use, while he was away

on a trip. To one man he gave five talents, to another two talents, and to the third one talent. The servant who had the one talent did not use it and said, "I was afraid, and went and hid thy talent in the earth . . . " (Matthew 25:25). A lot of people bury their talents because of fear. What was he afraid of? In my opinion, he lacked confidence in himself; he was also afraid because he did not feel he could make as big a showing as the others could make.

We constantly see people who have abilities and resources and opportunities beyond what we have. Then we have a tendency to pull back, because we cannot be as prominent as they are. This man with the one talent did not blame it on himself; he blamed his master, saying, " . . . I knew thee that thou art an hard man . . . " (v. 24). That was the excuse he used. Every person has some talent, but not every person uses that talent. It sometimes is much more comfortable to excuse away our failure.

5.   *Being "extremely sensitive" is another way we seek to overcome feelings of inferiority.* Study the people who lose their temper the quickest, who are the most easily offended, and you see what I mean. People who feel little, or defeated, or inadequate are the ones who get their feelings hurt, who pout, who build up feelings of being mistreated. Sometimes it is much easier to be resentful than it is to be resourceful.

6.   *Being "highly critical" is another method people use.* Not feeling equal among other people, we seek to cut them down to our size. We minister to our own conceits by picking out the flaws in others. Gossip is a form of exalting ourselves.

Three Good Methods

In a sense, all of us have some feeling of inferiority. But there are three legitimate ways that we can deal with it:

First, recognize that you are needed in the world. Recently, I was driving on a road in a rural community. I came to a place where the roads forked, but there was no sign there. There was a little store nearby, and I went over there and asked the direction to the place I wanted to go. There were four men in the store, and all four started at me at the same time. They felt a sense of superiority in being called on for help. That is always a stimulating experience. Every mother, social worker, physician, and every other person who serves people feels a sense of worth.

One of the turning points in the life of Saint Paul came in this way. He dreamed of going to Bithynia, but circumstances prevented him from going. He ended up in Troas, a place he did not want to be. Paul was disappointed. This could have been the end of his great ministry. Then, in a vision, he saw a man from Macedonia, and the man was saying to him, " . . . Come over into Macedonia, and help us" (Acts 16:9). That experience was really one of the turning points in Paul's life and in the history of the young Christian church.

There is some need in this world that every person can fill. I have a very close friend who has been extremely successful in his life. He told me that the turning point came when he was in high school. He was not making the highest grades in his class, and he felt defeated and unworthy. Then a wise teacher said to him, "Stop trying to be *the* best and start trying to be *your* best."

Maybe I cannot do as much as somebody else can, but at least I can do what *I* can. Recognizing that there is a place of service for me is a very stimulating experience.

It shall forever remain true, " . . . he that loseth his life for my sake shall find it" (Matthew 10:39). That is, you really find your greatest self when you find something greater than you are—something to which you can dedicate your life. You find your life by giving it away.

Second, we become important when we realize our possibilities. I picture in my mind a little baby and a little puppy playing together on the floor. The little puppy can run and jump. It can go over and drink water for itself and eat out of a plate by itself. In many ways, the little puppy seems the superior creature, but you look at the two, and you realize that that little puppy is going to grow up to be a dog—that little baby is going to grow up to be a woman or a man. The possibilities of that little puppy are very limited, but the possibilities of that baby are almost limitless. Recognizing that makes a tremendous difference in the valuation we put on each one of them.

The same is true of us. Any one of us can say that we might not be all that we want to be now, but we have *possibilities* of becoming far more than we are. In this connection, one of the statements Jesus made has been a tremendous inspiration to many people: " . . . to them gave he power to become the sons of God . . . " (John 1:12). Whoever we are, whatever we might have done, never forget that any and every one of us has the power to become—literally—the child of God.

There is an old song which says, "I'm a child of a king—a child of a king"—and truly we are.

Standing for something greater than ourselves is a third way of recognizing our possibilities and being our best selves. I read about a certain charm school, whose method includes having the student stand before a full-length mirror and repeat her name in a soft, gentle voice "so as to impress oneself with oneself."

That type of teaching produces characters like a girl I read about once. The author said of her, "Edith was a little country bounded on the north, and on the south, and on the east, and on the west by Edith."

There is the story of the two rooms: one of the rooms is lined with mirrors; the other room is lined with windows. In one room we only see ourselves; in the other room we see a great world, which is all around us. It is very important in which room we live our lives.

"Your Moment Has Come"

Right at this moment, I wish to emphasize two important truths:

1.   In "Pippa Passes," Browning wrote, "All service ranks the same with God." There are times when we feel so little and unimportant. But we need to remember that any service rendered in the right spirit is equal to any other service.

2.   For every person who is faithful in the living of each day, there will come an hour of destiny—a time of self-fulfillment. Many people feel frustrated and disappointed. But let me emphasize that no member of God's team trains for the race without one day being given a chance to run. Sooner or later, God says to every person who is ready, "Now—*now* your moment has come."

There is a purpose for every person, and as we give our lives as best we can to the opportunities which we have, we are certain to accomplish that purpose—and that is success in life. We *are* somebodies.

16
You Can Be What You Want to Be

When I was nineteen years old I was appointed the pastor of a church in Whitesburg, Georgia. At that time the population of that town was about two hundred and not much bigger than that today. When I went there to be the minister, I had never preached one sermon in my life. I had no theological training, and I really did not know how or where to begin. The few days before the first Sunday I was there, I worked on preparing my first sermon. It was on the prodigal son. I put down everything I could think of about the prodigal son, his father, and his elder brother, and then everything else I could think of about religion and the church. That Sunday I preached my sermon, and when I had finished, it was thirteen minutes long. I had told them all I knew.

Wise Advice

My father was a minister, and he lived not too far away. The next week I went to see him. I told him that it would be utterly impossible for me to be a preacher, because I could not get up enough to say. My father was a very understanding and kind man, but sometimes he could be very firm. He told me that if I *really* believed it, I could preach, and that by the end of that summer I would be as good a preacher as I ever would be the rest of my life. Somehow, I believed him, and I began to work at writing my sermons.

A few months ago, I was invited to preach to a conference of five thousand Christian leaders. I preached a sermon, verbatim, that I had prepared that first summer I was a minister. I now believe that sermon is as good as any sermon I have written in all the subsequent years.

Another fact my father told me, as I began as a minister, was that the *next* Sunday would be the most important Sunday for me, as a preacher. I have always believed that, and I have worked for next Sunday.

Today, I have the privilege of lecturing to many young ministers across the country. One of the points I keep telling them is that any one of them can be a good preacher—that he or she can start right now—and that next Sunday, "You can preach as good a sermon as you will ever preach the remainder of your life."

Start Now

I give this personal experience to say that whatever your dream is, whatever you want to do, whatever you want to accomplish, *you can do it.*

I am now thinking of a young lady who was married to a physician. They got a divorce, and she felt that her life was over. At the time she was twenty-eight years old, but she picked up the pieces and started over again. She went to college and studied premed; she went to medical school, and last year she graduated as a doctor of medicine. She is now beginning her career as a physician on her own. Many people in her position would have felt defeated, and that life was over.

If you wish to *be* somebody, stop putting it off until next week . . . or next year. You have to start now.

The most dangerous state in life is the point at which we are satisfied with who we are and what we are. In that state, we never listen, we are never responsive, we never dream. The first and the last word has already been spoken.

On the other hand, to be too dissatisfied and too unhappy

about yourself can also be harmful. It never accomplishes anything to keep denouncing yourself, and it is even worse when
we begin blaming other people for our troubles.

And furthermore, it is very easy to say that because of the
situation we are in, it is impossible to be and do that which is
in our hearts to do.

One only has to read the history of mankind to find out that
people who have been paralyzed or blind, or crippled, or suff-
ered from various physical illnesses have gone on to accomplish
high purposes in life. Sometimes we do things "on account of
" and sometimes we do things "in spite of."

On account of who you are, and the opportunities you have,
and in spite of the difficulties and problems you may face, you
can be that person.

Conditions for Becoming a Whole Person

To become a truly whole person there are several conditions
one must face. Let me mention just these:

1.　　　You must be just as willing *to give* as you are to *receive.*

2.　　　You must be as willing *to receive* as you are willing *to
give.* Some people's egos are fed by giving, but they feel
depreciated if they accept a gift.
Not long ago I said to one of my sons I would like to buy
him a suit of clothes. It made me feel good to buy him
that suit. The very next day, a man in the city where
I live phoned and said that he had been in contact with
a clothing store, and that I was to go by, pick out a suit
of clothes, and charge it to him, and accept it as a gift.
I thanked him, went and bought the suit, and enjoy
wearing it. The point is, I got joy out of giving a suit to
my son; I got joy out of a friend's giving me a suit. So
it goes in life.

3.　　　You must live by what you believe and not what you

disbelieve. In other words, you must live by what you are for and not by what you are against; or, to state it another way, you must live by what you admire and not by what you dislike.

4.   A fourth principle is to take life "for gratitude" and not "for granted." No person ever climbs the ladder of life without seeing the good happenings for which to be grateful. You begin with the rising sun in the morning, and all day long you see things for which you are grateful.

Many people do not think of what they can be or do; rather they spend their time being jealous of someone else; they gripe in bitter resentment. Jealousy of another person never accomplishes anything but giving you destructive emotions.

I have lived long enough and talked with enough people to know that the overwhelming majority of people have the abilities to be the people they want to be. But the ones that fail do so because of deficiencies in their own lives—lack of initiative; too little ambition; not being willing to take responsibility for oneself; dishonesty; and a lack of respect for other people.

A Special Rock

One of the greatest joys of my life is leading small groups of people on tours of the Holy Land. I have found inspiration in walking where Jesus walked that has truly blessed my life. He lived nearly two thousand years ago and His life seemed very simple. However, when anyone makes a list of the great lives that have been lived on this earth, he must begin the list with Jesus Christ.

One day, to get away from the multitudes of people, He went up on a mountain and sat down. I get very special inspiration every time I go up on the mountain where Jesus went. Once I

went to that mountain and walked around over it for a consid-
erable length of time. I kept asking myself, "If I wanted to sit
down for a time, where would I sit?" I finally selected a place
that appealed to me most. There was a large rock where *I* would
have sat. This rock weighs more than a hundred pounds. I got
a man to help me, and we brought that rock to Jerusalem. I had
it put in a box, got permission of the government in Israel to
bring it out of the country, and brought that rock home. It is
now on the altar of the church where I preach.

I have no idea whether it was the rock upon which Jesus sat.
I know it was the rock upon which *I* would have sat, if I had
walked up on that mountain. The importance of it is that certain of His disciples came to Him, and while He was sitting
there, He gave them the principles of life. These principles are
called "The Sermon on the Mount," and it can be read in the
fifth, sixth, and seventh chapters of Matthew's Gospel.

The Principles of Being the Person You Can Be

If you really want to know the principles of being the person
you can be, you need look no further. Here let me just quickly
lift up a few of these precepts, which the greatest person who
ever walked on this earth enunciated:

Blessed are the poor in spirit—that is, those who are not
conceited, who are not selfish.

Blessed are they that mourn—sorrows come; mistakes are
made; misfortunes happen. Happy is the person who truly regrets mistakes and wrongs, who sincerely sympathizes with
those who hurt.

*Blessed are they which do hunger and thirst after righteous-
ness*—that is, those who have ambitions and dreams and
desires. The person who never wants anything will never get
anything.

Blessed are the merciful—people who are too quick to judge
their fellowman—and too slow to forgive—eventually find
themselves condemned and unforgiven.

Blessed are the pure in heart—not only the wrong we do, but the wrong we *think* can sap the strength and power out of our lives.

Blessed are the peacemakers—learning to live peaceably with others, and helping others to live peaceably is one of the highest missions in life.

Blessed are ye, when men shall revile you, and persecute you —the path to the highest pinnacles of life is not covered with a soft carpet or a bed of roses. It takes struggle and hardship, but the reward is worth the cost.

These principles are just the beginning of what has come to be regarded as the summation of the highest and noblest teachings of all religions.

You can be what you want to be—if you learn and apply the right principles for your life.

17

You Never Find Happiness Through Searching for It

Every so often we hear or read the phrase *the search for happiness.* To me that is a contradiction within itself. In the Sermon on the Mount, to which we referred in the previous chapter, Jesus said, "Seek ye first the kingdom of God . . . " (Matthew 6:33). That is, determine for yourself a high purpose in living and give yourself to it. In another chapter Jesus said,

" . . . he that loseth his life for my sake shall find it" (10:39). Here it seems paradoxical, but it is true. You find happiness by forgetting about it. You find happiness by giving yourself to some other search.

Keeping on the Move

I would say, "Miserable are the persons who do not have something beyond themselves to search for." Searching means keeping on the move.

I grew up in the mountains of north Georgia, and I very happily remember the days when I could dip water out of a running stream in the mountains, and drink it without fear. The running water in the mountain streams was constantly purifying itself. Let the water reach a place where it quits moving, then it becomes stagnated, and impurities begin to develop in it.

Many of us can testify to the fact that one of life's most difficult experiences is the death of a loved one. When that experience comes, what do you do? One can sit around mourning in self-sympathy, or one can get up and get going. Again and again, we can find people whose lives reached their highest heights as they became active in the midst of a great sorrow.

The kind of people I like the best and I suspect that you do too are the "How are you?" type of people. That is, people who give me the feeling that they are not thinking about themselves, but their first concern is for me. As somebody reaches out in warmth and interest to another person—in the very reaching—one finds joy and satisfaction.

"Me-First" People

On the other hand, the people most of us dislike the most are the "What's in it for me?" folks. These "me-first" persons never feel warmth coming from any other person. You never find happiness when your favorite charity is yourself. Too many times we blame other people for our mistakes. When we are alone and lonely, it is too easy to say that everybody else marched off in the wrong direction, and we were the only ones to go in the right direction.

The people who forget themselves in thinking of others are the ones who say, "Let's go!" They never lack for fellowship and for friendship. The *me-first* persons are the ones who always end up being left out of the fellowship and the uplifting friendship.

In the Sermon on the Mount Jesus begins with happiness. The King James Version translates the word *blessed*. Really, that means happiness raised to its highest degree. It means happiness that is good for us. You can never be that person you really want to be, as long as you are unhappy.

The happy people enjoy their relationships with other people. The unhappy people dislike their work and their world. Sooner or later, they dissipate their talents and their gifts. Not finding satisfaction in work, one is never inspired to be or to do his or her best.

Faultfinding is the number-one temptation of unhappy people. Out of that come jealousy, self-depreciation, and even a hating of oneself.

Recently, I went to see a small child who was a patient in the hospital. It was about eight o'clock in the evening, when I went into the room. There sat the mother beside the child. I asked her if she had eaten dinner, and she replied that she had not. Then I asked her if she had eaten lunch, and again her reply was that she had not. What had happened was that she was so concerned with her child, that she forgot about her own hungers and her own needs.

When we find something important enough to give our full attention to, we quit worrying abour our own problems.

Signs of a Happy Person

Here let me sum up some of the signs of a happy person—those who take life "for gratitude" and not "for granted."

- The happy person lives by *affirmations* rather than *denunciations.*
- The happy person sees good in others. Read the four Gospels and you will not find where Jesus ever criticized a sinner. He did not approve of the sin, but He always affirmed people.
- The happy person gives wholehearted effort to some undertaking. Loafing on the highway never leads to happiness.
- The happy person is always eager to give, and also is willing to receive.
- The happy person knows that life is too short to be unhappy. Those who have experienced happiness universally testify that the other problems of life either disappear or else solutions are found.
- Finally, for the happy individual the problems of life are changed into challenges and opportunities.

18

Be the Boss of Your Habits

It can be said, "We live by our habits." When you are standing still and start to walk, you almost always will put one particular foot forward. Some start on the left foot, some on the right, but it's almost always the same foot for each person. When you put on your shoes, almost invariably you put on either the right or left shoe first. We are constantly performing acts unconsciously. We walk, we eat, we do so much of what we do by habit, without thinking about it.

There are habits of thought and habits of performance. In moments of excitement, some people habitually become very quiet, while others become very active. If they experience some defeat, or disappointment, or sorrow, some people retreat into their shells, while others become very expressive. Every person has many, many habits.

In reference to habits, we normally think first of such practices as tobacco, alcohol, some form of dope, profanity, criticism —that is, something evil, which enslaves us.

In reference to these enslaving habits, we need again to face the question "Who is boss?"

It might be painful, but it could be very profitable to sit down and make a list of the bad habits in our lives.

Dishonesty probably leads the list of human bad habits. Any one of us could very quickly make a list of a hundred ways in which a person can be dishonest. The tragedy is that dishonesty becomes a disease upon the soul of a person. Dishonesty can end up in self-hatred.

The worst social problem in our society today is alcohol. There are vast numbers of people who can "take it or leave it alone," but there is a growing number of people who have become enslaved to alcohol. They can "take it" but they can't "leave it." There are some people who are born apparently with some chemical mix in their body that causes them to be alcoholics from the first drink they take. There are others for whom alcohol becomes an almost unbreakable habit. That person is no longer free—instead he or she becomes an addict—a victim.

Six Basic Steps

Ironically, the steps in forming habits and in breaking habits are the same. There are six basic steps in making or breaking habits. They are:

1.   *Conviction.* This means that you have become convinced that you either want to form a new habit, or break an old habit. There is no wavering, no indecisiveness in your mind about it.

2.   *Your goal must be within your reach.* There are some good habits any one of us would like to develop, but we do not have the ability to do so. Likewise, there are some errors we would like to correct, but we have reached the point that our strength is insufficient.
     Once a man, in the bondage of some habit, went to a minister and said, "I do not believe in God, but if you do, for God's sake pray for me, for I need Him."

3.   *Preparation.* If you want to form a good habit, decide on the steps to take; likewise, in the breaking of a habit you have already formed. When you identify the habit and the procedure to follow, then you are ready to begin.

4.   *Begin.* Many good habits are never formed and many habits are never broken, simply because one keeps putting off the date of beginning. The longer the interval between the time when you make your decision and when you actually begin, the greater the difficulty you face. There is tremendous power which comes from the enthusiasm of a decision.

5.   *Keep going.* Once one has started on the procedure, persistence is absolutely essential. Exceptions destroy the entire process. No one can measure how many defeats have resulted from "just this once."

6.   *Satisfaction.* The satisfaction of accomplishment gives strength and stability that one has never realized before.

Greatest Accomplishment in Life

The greatest accomplishment in life is the mastering of one-self, and there is no deeper joy than to realize that you are living your life at its very best. The realization that you are improving brings self-confidence and maturity and strength and happiness.

Once a man promised his minister that he would never take another drink of alcohol. Late one night some weeks later, this man knocked on the minister's door and said to him, "If you do not release me from my promise to you and let me take a drink tonight, I will die."

The minister said, "Go home and die."

The next day the man visited the minister again with joy and triumph on his face. He said, "I died last night."

Four Kinds of Habits

In reference to habit, each of us can fit into one of four categories. Briefly, let us look at those:

1. There are people who have the habit of never attempting anything that is difficult. They have no heart, except for the easy task. They are interested only in merely getting by in life. These people start as late as possible and quit as early as possible. They give as little as they possibly can. Yet these same people wonder why others make progress, while they are held back.

2. The next group are persons who never hear what anybody else has to say. They never try to learn; they never observe; they are the "know-it-alls." It is always a disagreeable experience to be in the presence of a person who never hears any part of the conversation, except what he or she has to say.

3. Another group of people are those we call "the

fighters." They are against everybody and everything. They never see good in others, or in any institutions. In their thinking, the government is bad; the schools do not teach; the people who go to church are hypocrites; and on and on. They express their hostility at every opportunity. Someone has called such people "vicious wet blankets."

4.   Let us be thankful there is a fourth kind person who has developed the habit of looking for good in other people—who is willing to do more than is expected—who has developed the qualities of a lady or a gentle-man—who never puts people down, but is seeking to lift people up. This person is interested in making everything in the world better than it is.

Instead of hurting people, the habit of this person is to help. The glorious thing is that in lifting others up, this person is lifted up.

19
That Complex We Call Inferiority

The term *inferiority complex* has been applied to so many people in so many situations that it has almost lost its meaning. No one person can do everything as well as some other persons. I am fully aware that I cannot play a pipe organ, sing a solo, fix an automobile engine, set a broken leg, use the typewriter as efficiently as a secretary, interpret some legal question, balance my checkbook, and on and on. Every person I meet can probably do something better than I can do it.

However, recognizing my limitations is not the same as believing that I am inferior.

There are many things in life that I have no desire to learn or accomplish. On the other hand, recognizing my limitations in certain areas, I am encouraged to work harder toward accomplishment.

Inferiority Cover-ups

Feeling inferior, many people try to cover it up by such actions as bragging, loud talking, showing off, acting superior, and many other ways. Some of the loudest-talking people I have ever known, I have learned later were some of the most timid, inhibited people.

Sometimes people try to cover up their feelings of inferiority by seeking to drag down every person around them. Whenever you hear a person gossiping or engaging in any form of "character assassination," you may know that person is trying to cover his or her own feelings of inferiority. Belittling others is one way people try to increase their own size.

Reasons for an Inferiority Complex

1. *Measuring ourselves by somebody else's standards.* We are who we are, and the moment we start trying to be somebody else, the experience can be devastating.

2. *Never having learned how to face failures* is another pathway toward feeling inferior. As a boy, one of my heroes was Babe Ruth—the man who hit 714 home runs in baseball in the regular season. However, through the years it has been for me an encouraging fact to realize that as great a hitter as Babe Ruth was, he struck out more than twice as many times as he hit home runs. I long ago learned that I do not have to win every time.

3.   *Setting goals beyond one's ability can be very belittling.*
      This is one of the places where parents need to be very
      careful. Never compare your child with other children.
      Let each child stand on his or her own abilities and
      accomplishments.

How to Grow in Adequacy

Every person has feelings of inferiority, but every person can
develop the sense of adequacy.

1.   *Recognize that you, as one person, are important.* It is
      impressive to realize that just one vote accomplished
      the following: elected John Quincy Adams president;
      elected Thomas Jefferson president; elected Rutherford
      Hayes president; enacted military conscription in 1941;
      made California, Washington, Oregon, Texas, and
      Idaho states; beheaded Charles I of England; elected
      Oliver Cromwell; placed George I on the throne.
      Throughout history there have been numerous times
      when one person made *the difference.* Never let it be
      said that one person is not important.

2.   *Have someone you can talk to about your feelings.* The
      sharing of a feeling is the halving of a feeling. A feeling
      that can be shared loses half its power over your life.
      It is a wonderful blessing to have a friend with whom
      you can talk completely without reserve, realizing that
      what you say is safe and will never be passed on. One
      way to have such a friend is to be such a friend.
      In lecturing to young ministers today about counseling,
      one of the points I emphasize to them is that they may
      not be able to solve all the problems they hear, but they
      must be able to hold a confidence forever. To break a
      confidence is unworthy of any really decent person.

3.   *Accept your handicaps* without trying to cover them

up, make excuses for them, or let them belittle you. Undertake jobs that are within your ability. The success of accomplishment brings genuine satisfaction.

4. *Pick out something that you can learn and do well.* When you realize that there is at least one area in which you can work and be above average, it strengthens all of your other endeavors.

5. *Be careful not to be too sensitive.* In a sense we all react, but we must not let our feelings gain control over us. If we recognize that we are unequal to some task which we would like to accomplish, let us get acquainted with somebody who can help us. Near you there is someone who would feel flattered if you asked for his help. A cry for help is always a stimulating experience. In asking someone to help you, *you* not only gain assistance, but you help that person. Let us face the fact that our inadequacies can become adequacies, if we really apply ourselves to improving them.

6. *Control your emotions.* One of the most defeating experiences in life is to realize that your emotions caused you to say or do something which you did not really want to do or say. Feeling that we are not in control of our emotions is one of the most common causes of inferiority feeling. "Flying off the handle" is a belittling experience.

7. *Make a conscious effort to assert yourself.* You may decide on some skill that you want to develop, or some hobby which you can enjoy. Perhaps in conversation you need to be positive in expressing an opinion. There are many different ways of self-assertion, and when this is done, it builds confidence and opens avenues of self-development.

8. *Be sure you have the facts.* I know an attorney who is

considered to be extremely well qualified in the court-room. One day I asked him what he attributed his courtroom success to. He replied that whenever he went to court, he had so thoroughly studied the case and the law, that he was confident that whatever came up he could handle. The very moment we begin making statements of which we are not sure, then we begin to realize that we can be embarrassed or contradicted or belittled. When you know where you stand, you do not belittle yourself.

9. *When you "feel inferior," ask yourself if you do not feel physically below par.* Good health is one of the surest steps to a good opinion of yourself. It may be that you are violating some law of health; it may be that you have neglected a checkup by your doctor; it may be that you are not getting enough rest or eating the proper diet. Health greatly affects our feelings in every area of life.

10. *Finally, use your mistakes, instead of letting them use you.* There is tremendous power in looking at a mistake you've made, analyzing it until you understand the reason why you made that mistake, and studying it so that you feel confident you will never make that same mistake again. Instead of letting your mistakes get you down, be sure that you can gain mastery over them. Worry, remorse, a sense of guilt, embarrassment— these are all destructive and accomplish nothing. On the other hand, analysis, study, planning, positive ac-tion—these are constructive and uplifting.

What We Want the Most

I have talked with enough people to come to the conclusion that the three greatest desires of humanity are (as I pointed out earlier): *to be loved—to feel secure—to feel important.* I believe that most people put "feeling important" as the most important desire of their lives. We want to feel that we are counting for something.

Years ago, I read a survey taken to determine the most beloved poem among the American people. I do not have the survey before me, but I do remember the results. The third most popular poem among American people was William Cullen Bryant's "Thanatopsis." In that poem we read:

> So live, that when thy summons comes to join
> The innumerable caravan, which moves
> To that mysterious realm, where each shall take
> His chamber in the silent halls of death,
> Thou go not like a quarry-slave at night,
> Scourged to his dungeon, but, sustained and soothed
> By an unfaltering trust. . . .

That is a poem which speaks of confidence and courage, and we admire the spirit described there.

The second most popular poem among the American people was Samuel Walter Foss's poem, "Let Me Live in My House by the Side of the Road Where the Race of Men Go By." It is a poem that speaks of action and of service and of amounting to something.

The most popular poem in this survey was Longfellow's "Psalm of Life," in which he said:

> Let us then be up and doing,
> With a heart for any fate;
> Still achieving, still pursuing,
> Learn to labor and to wait.

Longfellow touches the spirit of people. We want to amount to something, to accomplish something. We want to feel important.

Many years ago there was a man named Stradivari. His greatest desire was to be an accomplished violinist. However, he did not have the talents to accomplish his dream. Instead,

he began to make violins. George Eliot wrote these words about
him:

> . . . When any master holds
> 'Twixt chin and hand a violin of mine,
> He will be glad that Stradivari lived,
> Made violins, and made them of the best . . .
>
> The masters only know whose work is good.
> They will choose mine, and while God gives them skill,
> I give them instruments to play upon—
> God choosing me to help him.

Stradivari might have felt inferior because he could not be
the violinist he wanted to be; instead, he did what he could do,
and from it he gained lasting satisfaction.

20
Finalize Your Fear

To some degree, fear is a plague to almost every person. Fear
is the basis from which most all of our other troubles arise.

We are afraid for our health, or that something might happen to a loved one, or that we might lose our money, or that a
war may come, and on and on.

We know that events are going to occur, but the reason we
fear is because we feel inadequate. Feeling unable to cope with
what *might* happen is the basis of anxiety. Here are a few
questions that you might ask yourself to test the extent of your
own fears:

Test Your Fears

1. Are there people that you hesitate to express your feelings to?

2. Do you have a tendency to brag, or exaggerate, or try to overly impress people?

3. Do you work hard but complain about how much you have to do?

4. Do you worry about what might happen tomorrow?

5. Do you feel equal to the life that you imagine you will have to live?

6. Do you feel that you measure up to what other people expect of you?

7. Do you often belittle yourself, hoping that the person to whom you are talking will contradict what you are saying and reassure you?

8. Do you find yourself belittling other people, seeking to lower them to the level where you think you are?

9. Are you given to excessive drinking of alcohol?

10. Are you constantly seeking praise, and do you feel depressed if you are not praised?

Yes answers to the above questions are real indications of inner fear.

Paranoia—Euphoria—Metanoia

Every person faces fear and, in facing fear, you have one of three choices as to the state in which you may live your life.

1. *Paranoia* is one state of living we may choose. It comes

from the word *paranous*. *Para* literally means *beside* and the word *nous* means *mind*.

Once the friends of Jesus felt that He was in this state and we read, "And when his friends heard of it, they went out to lay hold on him: for they said, He is beside himself" (Mark 3:21). The term "beside himself" is a common one. Sometimes we use the phrase "I was not at myself."

This is a state of mind when we are really not thinking correctly, or when we are not facing the basic and fundamental issues of life. In a sense, it is a means of escapism, when we flee from life's realities. Feeling inadequate in the face of some situation, many people do not face reality or attempt to deal with it in any meaningful way.

2.   *Euphoria* is another way that we can live, so as to escape our fears. Using this method, one is constantly seeking to make life simply fun and games. In a state of euphoria, one never takes life seriously; instead, one blissfully pursues pleasure in every possible way.

Once Ernest Hemingway expressed it in these words: "What is normal is what you feel good after."

We remember the Greek god Narcissus who fell in love with his reflection in the water. The word *narcissism* has become a common word in our language, and more especially, a common way of life among many people. It is the process of constantly doing that which brings pleasure, and escaping anything that might cause any pain.

This is not a new concept at all. We go back to the Book of Ecclesiastes and read, "I said in mine heart, Go to now, I will prove thee with mirth, therefore enjoy pleasure: and, behold, this also is vanity" (2:1).

From somewhere there came the expression "The life of Riley," and many people believe that if they can just achieve that, then all of their problems are solved.

There are times when it is wonderful to forget all the cares and worries of life, and just have a good time, but that is not the answer to the deep problems which beset our souls. Eventually, the laughter of euphoria becomes hollow and mirthless.

3. *Metanoia* is the third and right way of living to achieve life's greatest triumphs. Metanoia simply means the opposite of paranoia. It means to think clearly; to be in one's right mind; it means the restoration of common sense.

Biblical Example

Many of us believe that the greatest story ever told on this earth was the story that Jesus told of the prodigal son, which is found in Luke 15:11-32. In this story we have illustrated each of these forms of facing life.

First, "Father, give me the portion of goods that falleth to me . . . " (v. 12). He was not thinking straight; he was only thinking of today and was forgetting tomorrow. His only concern was with what he could get at the moment. He was "beside himself." The person who just thinks of today without planning for the future is not in a right state of mind.

Next we read, "And not many days after the younger son gathered all together, and took his journey into a far country, and there wasted his substance in riotous living." Here we have euphoria at its peak. His only interest was in having a good time. He was not thinking of any contribution he could make to improve his or any other life. His one concern was, "What can I do now that I enjoy?"

Then we read, "And when he came to himself . . . " (v. 17). That is the best definition of metanoia that one can find anywhere. He came to his senses. He began to think reasonably. To us this means recognizing the worthlessness of previous ways of life and facing life honestly, in spite of our fears.

Out of metanoia comes the experience of the prodigal son,

when he said, "I will arise and go to my father . . . " (v. 18). To us, this means we face the manner in which we have been living and are willing to change and live the right way. It is an about-face in the process of life. Not only does it mean a change of attitude; it means a change of actions. Here is repentance in its highest and finest form. Repentance does not mean mere sorrow for our past life; instead, repentance means a changed person and a new life.

God did not intend to deny the joys of life. When God made us, He made us with the possibility of laughter, but we are called to realize that we cannot simply laugh our way to the great heights of living. Fulfillment in life comes from facing life as it is, turning in the right direction, and resolutely marching forward.

Fear Can Be Conquered

One of the great spiritual experiences of all time is the one John Wesley had on board a ship at sea. A frightening storm arose, and it seemed that the ship would sink. Many people on board the ship were filled with fear. However, on the vessel was a small band of Moravians, and during the mighty storm they were calmly praying and singing God's praises. They exhibited no fear. Later John Wesley described the scene as follows:

> In the midst of the reading of a Psalm, the sea broke over and split the main sail in pieces, covered the ship, and poured in between the deck, as if the great deep had already swallowed us up. A terrible scream broke out among the English. The German Moravians calmly sang on. I asked one of them afterwards, "Were you not afraid to die?" And he answered, "I thank God, no." "But were not your women and children afraid?" He replied mildly, "No, our women and children are not afraid to die."

Wesley knew in that moment that he did not have that kind of faith. "I have a sin of fear," he wrote.

Let us make no mistake about it: the Christian faith indicates quite clearly that fear and anxiety can be overcome. Jesus said very implicitly "Take no thought for your life . . ." (Matthew 6:25). That is, do not be worried about tomorrow. He points out that there is an eternal God who created this universe, who knows the importance of your life, and who is able to meet every need. He tells us to set our lives toward some high purpose, and our other needs and wants in life will be given to us.

Whenever anxious and worried, one of the steps I take to overcome the feeling is to read that passage—Matthew 6:24-34. After reading that, I do all I can to fill my mind with that kind of faith.

Faith in God does not take away all the pain and suffering, but I believe as Tillich so well said when he spoke of this faith, "It does not build a castle of doubt-free security, but it does remove the fear to venture."

There is great inspiration in Van Dyke's wonderful poem "Voyagers":

> O Maker of the Mighty Deep
> Whereon our vessels fare,
> Above our life's adventure keep
> Thy faithful watch and care.
> In Thee we trust, whate'er befall,
> The sea is great, our boats are small.
>
> When homeward bound we gladly turn,
> O bring us safely there,
> Where harbour-lights of friendship burn
> And peace is in the air.
> We trust in Thee, whate'er befall;
> Thy sea is great, our boats are small.

21

Spite, Jealousy, and Self-pity

In one of his novels, C. S. Lewis said about a character: "Mark liked to be liked." That really is a profound statement, because it is one of the deepest feelings of every person. Small children crave attention and approval. Teenagers go through that period when they feel physically awkward and self-conscious. This leads to emotional insecurity and, above all things, the dread of becoming friendless. As we grow older, we naturally have a desire to be wanted, welcomed, esteemed, to be included by other people.

Liking to Be Liked

There is nothing wrong in liking to be liked. In fact, it is abnormal (and I believe even wrong), to not want to be liked. Over and over, we repeat the words of Jesus, "Thou shalt love thy neighbour as thyself." Loving yourself is right and good, and it equally applies to our relationship with other people.

The great Tolstoi wrote in his diary, "It is myself I am weary of and find intolerable. I want to fall asleep and forget myself and cannot." Nearly every person experiences feelings such as those, and when you feel that way toward *yourself,* you normally feel that way toward other people.

Liking to be liked (and not feeling that we *are* liked), drives us into the most unholy and unhappy moods, such as, spite, self-pity, and jealousy.

One of the most memorable experiences of my life was a

particular vacation that my wife and I spent. We landed at the airport in London with three weeks before us. We had no schedule; we had a rented car and carried a map of Great Britain. We knew nothing about the countryside, and we were not particularly concerned about where we went, so we started off. Whenever we saw something we liked, we would stop and look at it. We would spend the night at any place we found appealing. One of the realizations that impressed me the most during those three weeks was that I did not see one person I recognized, and no person recognized me. During those three weeks I did not need to worry about what anybody who might see me was thinking. They did not know me; I would soon be gone—and they would never see me again.

That was wonderful—for three weeks—and three weeks was about the right amount of time. We found ourselves ready to come back home to be among people we knew and who knew us, and to get back into the stream of life, where what we did and how we lived mattered, both to ourselves and to other people. Going through life, oblivious to other people, not being known and not knowing anyone is about the most miserable existence that any person could live.

Importance of Solitude

If there were only one person on the earth, that person could very likely find a very meaningful existence. It was Henry Thoreau who said that he had never found a companion so companionable as solitude. He went on to say, "A man thinking or working is always alone, let him be where he will." Moments of aloneness are very important and self-rewarding, and if we had never known any other person, I feel that any one of us could build a satisfactory life. However, living in a world of people, we not only are aware of those people, our lives are entwined with them. What somebody else does and says and thinks makes a tremendous difference to each one of us.

In order to get attention and acceptance people will go to

great lengths. Some people will pour out attention, praise, and, even flattery to any person around them who might accept it, feeling that in return they themselves would be accepted. On the other hand, there is the familiar expression "being given a cold shoulder." When that happens, some people retreat into lonely, self-depreciation. Self-pity is one of the most common means of excusing our own sense of lack of acceptance and sense of inadequacy. Self-pity retreats within itself.

On the other hand, the more aggressive response is spite and jealousy.

A Scapegoat

Many centuries ago, the Hebrews had a very unique way of atoning for their own sins and inadequacies. People would place a goat in their midst, and all of them would lay their hands upon it. They believed that as they touched the animal, their sins left them and were transferred to the goat. Then they would take sticks and beat the goat, driving it from their midst. As the goat went out of sight, the people felt that their sins were gone, and that they were purified.

This practice gave us our word *scapegoat.*

The tragedy of many people is that today they seek to make some other person a scapegoat. Feeling unworthy and unwanted, giving way to their jealousies and their spites and their self-pity, there is a tendency to make some other person bear the blame. We project our own unworthiness to make someone else the scapegoat. A man or a wife can blame the other; children can blame their parents; and in every area of life, we can always find somebody to make the scapegoat.

Here is where forgiveness comes in. Many times I have stood with groups of people and looked at a hill which might have been Calvary. On that hill you can see the outline of a skull, and we remember the words of the Bible, "And they bring him unto the place Golgotha, which is, being interpreted, The place of a skull" (Mark 15:22). I have watched hundreds of faces, as they looked at that spot and thought about the death of Jesus Christ. Almost spontaneously groups began to sing in a soft voice:

> On a hill far away stood an old rugged cross,
> The emblem of suff'ring and shame;
> And I love that old cross where the dearest and best
> For a world of lost sinners was slain.
>
> So I'll cherish the old rugged cross,
> 'Till my trophies at last I lay down;
> I will cling to the old rugged cross,
> And exchange it some day for a crown.
>
> GEORGE BENNARD

No wonder that hymn has been one of the most beloved hymns of all time. The cross is "God's scapegoat" for every one of His children.

This is what John the Baptist meant when he saw Jesus coming toward him and said, "Behold the Lamb of God, which taketh away the sin of the world" (John 1:29).

This is what Jesus meant when He ate that supper in the Upper Room with His disciples and then took a cup, saying, "...Drink ye all of it; For this is my blood of the new testament, which is shed for many for the remission of sins" (Matthew 26:27, 28). God gave us a remedy for self-pity, jealousy, and spite. Realizing the divine "scapegoat," we do not hate ourselves, and therefore we do not need to lash out at other people. We become both acceptable and accepting.

Understanding Acceptance

Understanding that God loves me, accepts me, and did die on the cross for me is my greatest safeguard against destructive behavior and my greatest inspiration to higher living.

Understanding my acceptance, I feel fit for service. Understanding my acceptance, I can love myself and, as a result, I can

love other people. Understanding my acceptance, I do not feel
that I must do things out of a sense of guilt. I am free to respond
in a sense of love. Let it be said over and over again, until it
sinks deeply into our minds—the only way a person can really
hurt you is to get you to hate him or her. One who understood
Jesus Christ quite well put it this way:

> [Love] suffereth long, and is kind; [love] envieth not;
> [love] vaunteth not itself, is not puffed up, Doth not
> behave itself unseemly, seeketh not her own, is not
> easily provoked, thinketh no evil; Rejoiceth not in
> iniquity, but rejoiceth in the truth; Beareth all things,
> believeth all things, hopeth all things, endureth all
> things. [Love] never faileth: but whether there be
> prophecies, they shall fail; whether there be tongues,
> they shall cease; whether there be knowledge, it shall
> vanish away.

1 Corinthians 13:4-8

22

Learn to Get Along With Others

This is one of the most necessary principles in living. It is
necessary in the home, in the school, in the neighborhood, in
the business, in the church. It is necessary wherever as many
as two or three people are gathered together.

"Love thyself." It is obvious that if one is happy, self-reliant,
filled with a wholesome self-respect, believes that he or she is

important, then that person easily desires the same things for other people.

On the other hand, if one feels guilt, remorse, shame, then that person naturally expresses hostility, finds fault, and blames somebody else. The suspicious, condemning person reveals his true inner self.

Three Attitudes

In order to live with and get along with other people, *we need to assume that they love us*. You have a right to believe that people ought to love you because of your very creation. You are God's child and you have a God-likeness. That does not make you conceited or cause you to think you are better than somebody else; the truth is the opposite. Believing you are God's child, you have a normal humility.

Assuming that people naturally love other people (as I believe normal people do), you will find it to be true.

A second attitude we must assume is *to really believe that each and every person merits our good will*. Again, this is true because of that person's creation. The most valuable asset in this universe is a human being. Some people do behave in manners that are less than lovable; even so, we can love persons, even if we do not approve of or like some of their actions.

A third attitude that is basic in living with other people is *to believe that within this universe there is a Power which is constantly loving us, and as you respond to the loving Power of the universe, you have a natural sense of well-being*. You become more and more a whole person.

Tensions in Marriage

Right at this point, there needs to be a few paragraphs in reference to marriage. At least half of all the problems I hear are those dealing with two people who are married to each other. As a result of counseling with many, many couples through the years, I have found that there are three main causes of tension and unhappiness in marriage.

1.   *Money.* There are many, many ways for a married couple to handle their money. The important thing is that they decide on a way with which both are pleased.

Being in debt can be one of the most destructive experiences in life. One of the tragedies of our society today is the ease with which people can get themselves almost hopelessly in debt.

As I mentioned earlier, many years ago, my wife and I decided that there were two things that we would never buy on credit—things we could eat up and things we could wear out. If a person buys a house, or makes investments on credit, that is a different matter. Having debts hanging over your head for things you have eaten up or worn out is a heavy burden to bear. Through the years, we never violated that principle, and we discovered that we could do without many things that at first seemed essential. I advise young married couples to avoid debt as if it were a plague.

Having a little savings account gives one a sense of security and serenity.

2.   *Family.* When a couple marries, they do not merely marry each other, they also marry each other's family. It is imperative that a person learns to appreciate and get along with the other's family.

On the other hand, it is equally imperative that the family learn to love and appreciate the person who marries into it. In every possible way, I must express loving acceptance of the ones my children marry.

3.   *Acceptance.* I well remember an experience which will never let me forget the importance of acceptance. I was speaking for several days in a small town. One day I was invited to lunch in a rather modest home. When I

got there, I could tell that they had made careful preparations for my coming. Everything in the house was perfectly in order; a lovely meal was prepared, and it was to be a very special occasion. Soon after I arrived, the husband came down the steps to greet me. He had on a purple shirt and an outlandish red tie. His wife saw him and said in a very harsh tone, "That is the ugliest tie you could have selected." I saw disappointment and hurt in that man's face. I realized that day that the worst tie that could be selected is not as bad as being criticized for wearing it.

Marriage is not a reformatory. We marry somebody, not because we think we can change them, but because we love them. Over and over, I say to people, "Accept each other as you are, and quit trying to change each other's faults."

Be Interested

Do you feel that people seek your friendship and fellowship? This is a very important question. Many people feel overlooked and left out. Here we need to emphasize the fact that the secret of being interesting is to *be* interested. Quit worrying about people's being interested in *you,* and start working to develop your own interests, as much as you possibly can.

I know a person (in fact we all know a person), who is interested only in himself or herself. In conversation, whatever subject you mention, this person is quick to top whatever you said with some personal experience. If you refer to a trip you made, the moment you pause, this person begins telling of a trip he or she made. If you refer to a member of your family, as soon as this person gets a chance, he or she will start telling you about a member of his or her family, and on and on. You get from such persons the idea that they are not interested in anything but themselves and their own concerns. Those people are avoided.

We can all remember times when we made mistakes, but happily we can remember times when we did the right thing. Such a time happened to me recently. I had dinner with a couple who had recently been to Europe. They were obviously excited about their trip. This was their first trip out of the country, and the first long airplane ride they had ever had. During our dinner and for almost an hour afterward, they told me every detail about their trip and I listened—at times with interest and at times with boredom—but I *listened,* and I am very pleased with myself that I did.

It would have been so easy for me to break in and say, "Let me tell you about the last time *I* was in Europe." They wanted somebody to listen, while they told about the trip of their lives. And really, I did find it interesting to see what a couple would say about their first trip abroad.

Importance of Listening

Parents need to remind themselves constantly that children need to be listened to. A father recently told me of an experience with his son. This son had finished college and had gone to work in a large corporation. In his work he was having some difficulties adjusting to his fellow workers, as well as learning his job. One night the son said to his father, "I wish you would advise me about my situation." The father told me that for almost two hours the boy sat and talked to him about both the problems and the possibilities in his situation. Patiently, and with genuine interest, the father listened, as the boy talked. Finally the boy finished and said to his father, "You have really helped me tonight and I feel that everything is going to work out fine."

The father hardly said a word, but sometimes listening is more powerful than speaking. Listening to a person is the very essence of counseling. Most people do not want you to give them advice. They want you to listen to *their* ideas. If you are willing to listen, you have laid the foundation of lasting friendship.

I repeat: *the trouble with many people is that they have never extended their interests beyond themselves.*

What Are Your Interests?

It is a good thing to sometimes take pencil and paper and make a list of your interests such as:

1. Yourself

2. Your family

3. Your city, state, and country

4. The affairs of the world

5. Sports

6. Cultural interests

7. Religion

8. Politics

9. Scientific developments

10. Literature
(Add additional subjects that interest you.)

As you make your own list, be honest about it. Are you really interested in these things which you are writing down? How much time and effort do you give in developing your interests?

Remember this: as you broaden your interests you will find more people to be interested in you.

A Personality Interest Checklist

In living happily and harmoniously with other people, we must begin with ourselves. Here let me suggest a checklist in six areas of your life. Rate yourself from one to ten. When you finish, add up your scores and divide by the number you rated. Seven is usually a passing grade. If you rate below seven, then you need to get busy on yourself.

1. **APPEARANCE**
   Neatly dressed
   Careful about bodily cleanliness
   Physical posture
   Facial expression

2. **EXPRESSION**
   Tone of voice
   Limit of vocabulary
   Enunciation of words
   Use of slang
   Correct grammar
   Talk too much
   Talk too little
   Enthusiasm

3. **INTELLIGENCE**
   Superstitions
   Rationalizing one's actions
   Intellectual honesty
   Knowing the facts before giving an opinion
   Memory for names
   Attentiveness
   Observing

4. **EMOTIONAL CONTROL**
   Control of temper
   Feeling of jealousy
   Sense of humor
   Too sensitive
   Stingy
   Generous
   Self-pity
   Moody

5. INTERESTS
    Reader of books
    Reader of newspaper
    Variety of listening on television and radio
    Variety of movies
    Cultural development
    Concern for people
    Religious convictions

6. SOCIAL ADAPTING
    Tolerance
    Prejudices
    Amount of showing off
    Should assert yourself more
    Should assert yourself less
    Feeling of sympathy
    Sarcastic
    Praise for other people
    Willingness to serve

The above subjects, if carefully studied and applied to ourselves, can be very revealing, both as to our failures and our possibilities.

Rules For Getting Along With Other People

Here's a brief summary of what we have been discussing in this chapter.

1. Be interested in the happiness and well-being of other persons, and be sympathetic with the hurts and problems of other persons.

2. Learn the names of people.

3.   Do not speak with an uncontrolled temper.

4.   Be careful to greet persons when greeting is in order.

5.   Be slow to condemn, quick to praise.

6.   Be willing to give more than you ask from others.

7.   Forgive and be willing to ask for forgiveness.

8.   Believe that you are making some important contribution to life.

9.   Believe that each person you meet is making some important contribution to life.

10.   Remember, no person is big enough to cause you to hate.

11.   When disagreements arise, do not concentrate on fixing blame, but rather, concentrate on communication.

12.   Seek to understand the right action in each situation—and then do it.

Conclusion: Why Jesus Came

Jesus said, " . . . I am come that they might have life, and that they might have it more abundantly" (John 10:10). Abundant *living!* That is what the Christian faith is all about. In summary, let me give four essentials for abundant living:

1.   *Man in essence is spiritual.* It is true that we are physi-

cal bodies and we live in a physical world, but the substance of life is that which you and I recognize as spiritual. This leads inevitably to the conviction of immortality. The very foundation of life is that there is something in us beyond the physical, which lives forever.

We cannot prove the spiritual dimensions of a person, so we accept them on faith. Donald Hankey of England said, "Believing in eternity means betting your life on God."

This is the first step to true abundant living.

2. To be our best—to get the most out of life—*there are certain moral standards, which must be faced.* Within us is a sense of "ought." Moral standards vary according to society, culture, environment, our religious teachings, and our upbringing; but within all of us, there is a feeling that some things are right and some things are wrong.

    Those who have been reared in the Christian faith realize that the highest standard of life is in Christ. He does not want to restrict us or restrain us. Across the years, many of us have had problems with these so-called "list" Christians. Many of us grew up hearing people say that to have a good life you need to not smoke, not drink, not dance, not play cards, not buy things on Sunday, and so forth. We heard the old song, "I don't smoke, I don't chew—I don't go with the girls who do." But that is not the Christian faith. The Christian faith is a positive, uplifting experience. *Jesus gives us a life to live, not a set of things not to do.* And in living that life, we find "an abundance."

3. As we study the life of Christ, we find that He goes far beyond the *dos* and *don'ts,* and gives us both the inspiration and the tools of abundant living. *In the Christian faith we learn how to love and pray and believe and forgive and to overcome.* We learn that living is not

reciting a creed or going through a ritual—there is a life to be lived.

4. Finally, *we gain abundant living through being in an environment that makes it possible*. This is why the very first Christians gathered themselves together in a fellowship, and out of that fellowship came the church. To live abundantly, it is required that we have a sense of community—that we have love relationships with other people. Abundant living comes not merely through thriving, but rather through being in an environment and relationships which are uplifting.

A young man who had left home for the first time wrote to a minister friend of mine, saying that he was living in a terrible environment. He described the degrading influences that he was subjected to constantly. He ended his letter with the question, "How can I keep on being a Christian, living where I am?"

The minister very wisely wrote to him, "You probably will not. Therefore, move."

I am come that you might have life, and that you might have it more abundantly. Living in the fellowship of committed people makes abundant living much more reachable.

These are the four essentials.

This is a complete list of books by Charles L. Allen since he became a Revell author in 1951.

GOD'S PSYCHIATRY
THE TOUCH OF THE MASTER'S HAND
ALL THINGS ARE POSSIBLE THROUGH PRAYER
WHEN YOU LOSE A LOVED ONE
WHEN THE HEART IS HUNGRY
THE TWENTY-THIRD PSALM
THE TEN COMMANDMENTS
THE LORD'S PRAYER
THE BEATITUDES
TWELVE WAYS TO SOLVE YOUR PROBLEMS
HEALING WORDS
THE LIFE OF CHRIST
PRAYER CHANGES THINGS
THE SERMON ON THE MOUNT
LIFE MORE ABUNDANT
THE CHARLES L. ALLEN TREASURY (Charles L. Wallis)
ROADS TO RADIANT LIVING
RICHES OF PRAYER
IN QUEST OF GOD'S POWER
WHEN YOU GRADUATE (with Mouzon Biggs)
THE MIRACLE OF LOVE
THE MIRACLE OF HOPE
THE MIRACLE OF THE HOLY SPIRIT
CHRISTMAS IN OUR HEARTS (with Charles L. Wallis)
CANDLE, STAR AND CHRISTMAS TREE (with Charles L. Wallis)
WHEN CHRISTMAS CAME TO BETHLEHEM (with Charles L. Wallis)
CHRISTMAS (with Charles L. Wallis)
WHAT I HAVE LIVED BY
YOU ARE NEVER ALONE
PERFECT PEACE
HOW TO INCREASE YOUR SUNDAY-SCHOOL ATTENDANCE (with Mildred Parker)
THE SECRET OF ABUNDANT LIVING

CHRISTIAN HERALD ASSOCIATION AND ITS MINISTRIES

CHRISTIAN HERALD ASSOCIATION, founded in 1878, publishes The Christian Herald Magazine, one of the leading interdenominational religious monthlies in America. Through its wide circulation, it brings inspiring articles and the latest news of religious developments to many families. From the magazine's pages came the initiative for CHRISTIAN HERALD CHILDREN'S HOME and THE BOWERY MISSION, two individually supported not-for-profit corporations.

CHRISTIAN HERALD CHILDREN'S HOME, established in 1894, is the name for a unique and dynamic ministry to disadvantaged children, offering hope and opportunities which would not otherwise be available for reasons of poverty and neglect. The goal is to develop each child's potential and to demonstrate Christian compassion and understanding to children in need.

Mont Lawn is a permanent camp located in Bushkill, Pennsylvania. It is the focal point of a ministry which provides a healthful "vacation with a purpose" to children who without it would be confined to the streets of the city. Up to 1000 children between the ages of 7 and 11 come to Mont Lawn each year.

Christian Herald Children's Home maintains year-round contact with children by means of an *In-City Youth Ministry*. Central to its philosophy is the belief that only through sustained relationships and demonstrated concern can individual lives be truly enriched. Special emphasis is on individual guidance, spiritual and family counseling and tutoring. This follow-up ministry to inner-city children culminates for many in financial assistance toward higher education and career counseling.

THE BOWERY MISSION, located at 227 Bowery, New York City, has since 1879 been reaching out to the lost men on the Bowery, offering them what could be their last chance to rebuild their lives. Every man is fed, clothed and ministered to. Countless numbers have entered the 90-day residential rehabilitation program at the Bowery Mission. A concentrated ministry of counseling, medical care, nutrition therapy, Bible study and Gospel services awakens a man to spiritual renewal within himself.

These ministries are supported solely by the voluntary contributions of individuals and by legacies and bequests. Contributions are tax deductible. Checks should be made out either to CHRISTIAN HERALD CHILDREN'S HOME or to THE BOWERY MISSION.

Administrative Office: 40 Overlook Drive, Chappaqua, New York 10514
Telephone: (914) 769-9000